AF366932

JESUS CHRIST IN LOVE

(A Book of Poems)

Interpretation of the Messiah's early teachings

Dr Antony Theodore

Edited by

Dr Tapan Kumar Pradhan

The poems included in this volume are purely creative works of art based on the author's personal experiences. Unless otherwise indicated, all the names, characters, businesses, places, events and incidents mentioned in this book are either the product of the author's imagination or used in a fictitious manner. Any resemblance to actual persons, living or dead, or actual events is purely coincidental.

This book is being sold with the condition that it shall not, by way of trade or otherwise, be lent, re-sold or otherwise circulated without the prior consent of the publisher. No part of this book may be reproduced or copied in any form by any means   or reproduced on any disc, tape, digital media or other information storage devices etc without the written permission of the publishers.

Copyright © 2019 Kohinoor Books
All rights reserved.

ISBN : 978 – 81-942835-3-9

First Edition 2019

published and marketed by

KOHINOOR BOOKS
www.kohinoorbooks.com

Kohinoor Star Publications Private Limited
2293-A, REC Road, Mancheswar Rail Station
Bhubaneswar – 751 017

CONTENT

PART-I :- Miracle of Birth

PART-II : Word of God

PART-III : Mystery of Love

PART-IV : Voyage of Life

PART-V : Temptation of God

PART-VII : The After Life

EPILOGUE

ACKNOWLEDGEMENT

I owe a deep debt of gratitude to my fellow poet friends on Poemhunter website. My poetic craft has been shaped by the honest feedback received from thousands of readers. Although I have published my poems online on several websites, it is on poemhunter.com that I received wholehearted support from many kindred souls.

Dr Tapan Kumar Pradhan offered to present my poems in a book form. Many years ago I had requested Dr Tapan to write a few poems for me. I had also once requested him to gift a book of his choice to me. He had promised to me both. I think he has far exceeded my expectations. I have discussed with him several of my poems at length. I have also discussed with him the underlying unity among all the major religions of the world including Christianity, Hinduism and Islam. I believe that he shares my thoughts on the relevance of Christ's teachings for the modern world. I have full faith in his capacity to honestly interpret my poems.

ANTONY THEODORE

FOREWORD

This book contains 196 poems under seven different parts. All the poems are themed on Jesus Christ and his teachings. But the book is not on Christianity. Rather the book explores the universal truths in Christ's teachings which are applicable to every human civilization in all ages.

The largest part of the book is on Love. Although Jesus Christ's entire life was an embodiment of universal love, his teachings also covered various aspects of intimate human love as lay persons understand it. According to the poet, the natural attraction between man and woman is a reflection of the universal love force immanent in all creation. Marriage is not only a holy sacrament, but also a divine form of worship. True love finds fulfilment through the covenant of marriage. Breaching of that covenant is a breach of man's eternal relationship with God.

Antony Theodore is a spiritual poet. Although he has written extensively on the scriptures of all major world religions, his meditations on Christ have been most revealing and uplifting.

Antony has written thousands of poems in different languages. Many of these poems are already scattered over the internet in various forms. This book is a humble attempt to bring the best amongst all those poems under a single comprehensive organised framework. I have selected these poems on the basis of their immediate relevance to the broad theme and structure of this book. These need not be the most representative of Antony's immense poetic oeuvre.

In many of the poems included in this books, the poet has provided footnotes to throw light on the conceptualisation as well as the scriptural and historical background of the theme. Occasionally I have provided additional notes to drive home the spiritual undertones of a poem. My notes essentially contain my views, and need not reflect the poet's original view on the matter.

Many of the poems have been edited by me to conform to the overall design of the book. Some poems were originally in free flowing passage form. These have been modified and tweaked slightly so as to have a more presentable verse form. Some abbreviations have been expanded and some unclear words have been removed. However the original essence has not been compromised with. I have been in close correspondence with the poet for almost a decade. I have discussed both poetic techniques as well as scriptural interpretation with the poet over hundreds of fruitful hours. So I have reason to believe that I understand the poet's point of view behind these creations. I am thankful to the poet for allowing me the liberty to freely explore and interpret these spiritual gems.

Some of the poems contained in this book have appeared in slightly different versions on various websites and online platforms. Antony has also been editing and tweaking her poems online from time to time. However, I am presenting the poems as received by me from the poet during my extensive correspondence with the latter.

EDITOR

ANTONY THEODORE
Life and Works

Readers worldwide have been intrigued by Dr Antony Theodore's inspiring poems on humanity, religion and spirituality. Antony's poems offer amazing clarity and insight into many cryptic messages contained in world scriptures such as Bible, Gita, Veda and Quran. The poems are very simple but original, and they contain the underlying essence of all world religions. Antony does not preach any particular doctrine. But rather the poems contain universal messages of brotherhood and love.

Who is Antony Theodore?

Dr Antony Theodore has legions of followers on various online poetry platforms. On Poemhunter website Antony is one of the topmost popular poets in the English speaking world. Thousands of poets and readers worldwide have read and commented on the unique and insightful spiritual gems penned by "Antony Theodore".

According to legends and hearsay Dr Antony was born as John Antony Theodore Vazhakoottathil in Alleppey district of Kerala, India. After he was orphaned in early childhood, he was nursed by his devout Catholic godmother Genova Ma. After Genova's untimely demise Antony migrated to Germany. He studied at Ludwig Maximilian University in Munich and Fordham University in New York. He reportedly obtained two bachelor's degrees in science and business administration, and later on obtained two doctoral degrees in English literature and Philosophy of World Religions.

In 1986 when he was travelling from India to Germany, Antony's flight carrying 400 passengers got hijacked at Karachi airport in Pakistan. He survived with four gunshot wounds, while 22 of his fellow passengers were killed in the 17 hour long siege. This traumatic experience turned his mind to poetry and social activism. He was ordained as a pastor and served as a chaplain in St Martin, Munich. Antony remained unmarried and spent a large part of his life in Dortmund, Germany.

However, the diligent and inquisitive readers might have already guessed that actually there is no such poet as the Christian Poet Dr Antony Theodore in the physical world in the 21st century. There is no such poet in Germany as claimed in many websites. One Fr Antony Theodore is listed in the Diocese of Alleppey, and one Pastor Antony Theodore Vazhakoothathil in listed in the pastoral team of Dortmund. The list of persons injured in the 1986 Pan Am flight hijack at Karachi (en route to Frankfurt from Mumbai) also contains a person named Father Anthony Theodore. However none of these persons correspond to the poet writing under the pseudonym of Dr Antony Theodore aka Tony Brahmin on Poem Hunter and myriad other poetry websites. When I first came across Antony's poems on internet, I did extensive search online to identify the person. A careful scrutiny of the poems clearly points to the poet's Indian roots and family connections with the Kashmir province of India.

Hemangi Sharma as Tony Brahmin

Dr Antony Theodore is none other than the Indian mystic poet Hemangi Sharma. This is a truth which was known only to me till date. This is because Hemangi Sharma never liked to publish poems under her own name. She has various reasons for doing so. Hemangi has written thousands of poems under hundreds of different pseudonyms such as Lalitha Iyer and Poet Poet etc. Antony Theodore is her pseudonym or fake ID under which she has published her interpretation of Jesus Christ's universal teachings on Poemhunter platform. In routine online correspondence with fellow poets Antony Theodore invariably uses the nickname Tony Brahmin, which reflects Hemangi Sharma's Indian origin as someone born in a traditional Kashmir Brahmin family.

The Epilogue to this book contains details of Hemangi Sharma's poetic works under various pseudonyms on poemhunter and other websites. Further details on Hemangi Sharma's extraordinary relationship with me can be found in my book *I, She and the Sea*.

What is Antony's Religion?

Antony Theodore primary writes on Christian values. In her poems the birth, wanderings, teaching, suffering, crucifixion and resurrection of Jesus Christ have been tellingly re-enlivened. However "Antony" does not profess any particular religion. Her poems bring forth the universal truths common to all world religions. Antony is as much a Hindu and Muslim as she is a Christian, Buddhist and Confucian.

INTRODUCTION

Jesus in his physical human form graced this earth for a brief period of thirty three years at the beginning of the modern Christian era. The four books of the New Testament of Holy Bible throw light on only the birth, infancy and the last few years of his ministry. The Gospel is silent on the intervening years of Jesus's extraordinary life. However the record of his teachings as gleaned from those few years of his life have had a profound impact on the shaping of world history. The momentous impact of that one human life is still being felt in the unfolding of human civilisation. That extraordinary impact emanates from the purity, truth and love manifested in the unblemished life of Christ.

Jesus used to speak to his disciples in the ancient Aramaic language. The teachings have been carried forth by the apostles and missionaries to the furthest corners of the world in several different languages. The teachings have been translated and re-translated hundreds of times, finally culminating in the authorised King James version, which is the most widely accepted today. However, much of the original teachings have been distorted and lost through the translations.

For instance, we may take the expression "Word of God". Its exact equivalent in Vedic Sanskrit is "Shabda Brahman" – i.e. Word-God. It may be noted that Shabda in Sankrit has two meanings – Word as well as Sound. In the original Aramaic version, Word of God would have symbolised the primordial sound of creation (Aum-Amen-Amin) which permeates the entire universe. However, translated into modern English, Word merely connotes the written word as a combination of letters of the alphabet. If we take the original meanings, we shall find that all the scriptures of world religions essentially speak the same One Truth.

Similar is the case with other Biblical expressions like Bread, Wine, Fish, Star, Flesh etc. In the original Aramaic the meanings would have been quite different from what they ordinarily connote today. The present book does not attempt to dig out the original meanings through phonetic or lexical re-interpretation. It merely acknowledges that the inner meanings of the scriptures can be quite different from the surface meaning of the text.

Antony Theodore's poems delve much deeper than the surface meaning of Biblical teachings. Rather they dwell on the universal message of love and brotherhood contained in the Gospel, which is the same as that expressed through the Vedas, Gita, Quran and other world scriptures.

The poems in this volume have been arranged under seven parts. These broadly correspond to different phases of Jesus' life on earth juxtaposed with various stages of human development from infanthood through life's struggles and final deliverance from worldly delusion.

The poem "I Am Your Baby, Mum" by Antony Theodore has been translated into more than twenty different world languages. This has been reproduced in the first part of this book under the title "Mother". This opening part titled "Miracle of Birth" describes certain events associated with Jesus' miraculous conception and birth through the virgin mother Mary. On a metaphysical level this symbolises birth of the desire for emancipation taking root in the adult human heart. The "baby" in this book represents the nascent spiritual aspirations in the devotee's heart.

The second part of the book dwells on the Word of God. The scriptures of all world religions have sung the glory of the primordial cosmic sound which is indistinguishable from the concept of God in all religions. The one sound is known as Aum, Amen, Hum and Amin in different religions. On metaphysical level, awareness of the Word indicates man's awareness of his oneness with the cosmic absolute. The poems "Bread of Life" and "Make Me Thy Water, Lord" are allusions to Christ's assertion that man shall not live by bread alone but by the power of Word. The cosmic sound has been described by many sages as the "sound of many waters".

The third part deals with human emotion of love. By loving another human being one expresses love for the Supreme Lover who is present in all hearts. Union of a man and woman through marriage sacrament is a mundane expression of that divine love. In the poem "Come With Me, Elope" the poet is as if coaxing the reader to escape into the waiting arms of the Cosmic Beloved. "My Flesh Pines For You" expresses the same divine longing. This Part-III is the largest section of the book. This is also Antony's favourite subject area since he uses colourful imagery to describe the ever new mysteries of human love.

The fourth part describes the journey of Jesus across many lands. This symbolises man's mundane journey through many experiences of life. These experiences are perceived through the five senses of sight, sound, smell, taste and touch. The poem "A Tortoise Taught Me" teaches us that much more knowledge can be gained through interiorisation of one's senses (withdrawal of limbs like tortoise) as compared to the superficial knowledge gained from sense organs.

The fifth part deals with temptation of the flesh or allurement to senses during worldly life. Temptation basically means awareness of duality in existence, which is Satan as per Christian belief and Maya as per Hindu tradition. Due to worldly temptation one perceives the ego as distinct from God, and it primarily results from attachment to sense organs. By rising above all earthly temptations one can perceive the non-duality or oneness of all existence.

The sixth part describes Christ's suffering on the cross as a prelude to his grand eternal freedom in God. The wooden cross has multiple layers of spiritual meanings. It signifies the crossroads of human existence between the mundane and the sacred. It also symbolises the suffering of man through attachment to senses – the outstretched limbs indicating life energy flowing outward through sense organs. The killing of human attachment to sense organs on the symbolic wooden cross is a prerequisite for ascension to heaven.

The last part dwells on the possibilities of eternal life on the earth and beyond. The suffering multitude is waiting for the Second Coming of Christ for redemption. It is believed that the second coming will not be a physical resurrection of the human body of Jesus, but rather a spiritual awakening within each human being. This is the very essence of Antony's poetry. These timeless poems call out to the readers to shed their limiting individual ego and to merge themselves completely in the eternal bliss of God realisation.

PART - I

THE MIRACLE OF BIRTH

JESUS IN THE MANGER

AND A BABY IS BORN

Truth is naked. Truth was, is and will ever be. But we humans like to wear masks.

To perceive pure love that is God, you have to unmask your heart, unmask your soul, unmask the purity of your being.

Mind, reasoning and all sensory knowledge are only stumbling blocks in realising the pure purity of being. When you realise this simple truth, you give up all thinking. And when you give up thinking the ugly clothing will fall down. The naked cabaret dancer will start dancing. Beauty will flow, hearts will smile, penetrating your being with knives and organs made of pure energy. Then a little baby you will become. Like amoeba, you are the mother, you are the kid.

For when God's light opens my heart, I hear the laughter of innocence in my being.

MOTHER

I am your baby Mum.
I did not come on my own Mum.
God's angels flew down to your womb
From the mighty heavens
And placed me in your holy womb.

I did not come on my own mum;
God wanted it so.

I was so happy in my new cave of love
In your holy womb
And slept there peacefully.
The angles watched.
They prayed
To keep me safe always
Till I will be born on the face of the earth.

They practiced heavenly songs of birth
to play on their golden harps on my birthday.

When I was sleeping in your womb
The angels used to come to me.
You did not know it, my dearest Mum.

I was happy to be born
as your beloved child.

I wanted to smile
I wanted to sing
I wanted to play
I wanted to suck your breast milk

Until you were satisfied.
I wanted to see the smile on your face
When I suck all your milk from your loving breasts.

They were my dreams in your womb, Mum.

But on a cruel day
you decided to kill me.

The devils in the Hades
heard about your decision.
They brought the loudest drums
played in the devilish rhythms.
All the devils came together,
came and danced in circles,
jumping and singing.
They danced in lines.
They danced in circles.
They danced on the toes.
They danced on their heads.
They sang the wildest of songs
and the devil drummers played.
The whole hell was happy
that you decided to kill me.

You know how much I cried?
You know how many angels cried?
Do you know how the whole heaven cried
on my day of death in your holy womb?

A moment before i was cruelly murdered
I saw the All-Powerful God crying helplessly.

MY HEART IS OUTSIDE ME

When my Mum made a decision
to become pregnant
she began to love me
and I felt that love
for I am her own flesh and blood.

It was her decision, forever
to have her heart
go walking around
outside of her own body

Later as I grew up
I asked my mum:
"Tell me mum how did you feel
while carrying me within?"

And she answered me:
"The joy, honor, gift, and privilege
of being a mum is tremendous

From the second I felt
the tiny, indelibly precious
delicious, indescribable movements
when I heard my child's first heartbeat
to experiencing the first breath
becoming a mum is truly
a celebration of motherhood.

In grace and love I did everything
seeing you my own flesh in my soul

I saw heaven every single day
when you smiled, played,
rested happily on my breasts

You are all mine and I felt
My heart was outside of me.

CHICK BECAME AN EAGLE

Beyond the world of the skies
in unending heights
there lives Love
in the high holy temple.

At dusk, in the mild mystic light,
when the day and night kiss
only for a moment as their fate is,

Love came to the gates
of the holy temple
to climb down
steps innumerable.

At the end of the steps
stood I like a shivering chick
in utter darkness.

Love came to me,
arms widespread
breaking the shells of my loneliness
to cradle my whole being.

Ecstasies came !! Courage filled my veins !!

Love shook me out of fear,
and cured my inner wounds.

Love is all that I am.
Love came to set me free.

In the flush of love's light
I become bold
and take my flight,
into the world of delight.

It was the flight of an eagle.

(Poet's Note :- love alone can transform a shivering chick into an eagle. Mixing up of tenses
here is intentional.)

THE SEAL OF GOD

My mother told me
that angels carry
the seal of the living God
they want to put the seal
on the forehead
of the servants of God.

Today I had a dream
I saw a great multitude,
from every nation
race, people and tongue
lining up in hordes
before the golden throne
of the Almighty

Each had a white dove in the hand.

And then came the deluge
History was re-written
in dazzling letters of gold
God hugged each of them
all those who survived
the times of great distress
and withstood all temptations.

God made them wear
pure dazzling white robes
washed clean by the angels

Then the angels came
and put the seal of God
on their foreheads

I saw their happy shining faces
touched by angels and hugged
by the Almighty.

TODAY I AWAIT

Last night I waited for you
On my knees I remained
thinking of you my Lord.

Did you come to me
when I fell asleep
during my prayer?

When I woke up
I did sense
the wondrous smell of roses
which angels threw on your path

When I got up
I did feel the presence
Someone came to me in my sleep
to cut away with a sharp sword
all my selfish desires and thoughts

Was it you who came?
Was it you, my Lord?

MY RED UMBRELLA

With my red umbrella
I stood alone in the rain
in my secret garden
crying behind my umbrella
imploring for mercy
for all the sins I committed.

This Christmas day
when Jesus is born
the innocent baby
in utter poverty
I cry behind my red umbrella.

Oh I love your birth
I kneel before you
O Lord of the universe,
forgive me my sins
of aborting my own children

Many a time i did
this horrible sin
I hear them crying
in my sacred womb.

Baby my beloved one
in Bethlehem,
forgive me
forgive me
forgive me.

i am hiding now
under my red umbrella,
symbol of the blood
of my babies i poured
inside my womb.
forgive me Lord
forgive me.

BEAUTIFUL BUTTERFLY

O beautiful butterfly
Your face comes so true to me

Through a pretty butterfly
You come flying so serene into me

As the tiny wings flutter
I watch with love and joy
and wonder how it could be
I see your face coming to me

With beauty and grace
you perch among flowers
as if searching for a special place
If I could only turn my heart
into a bed of flowers
for you to fly and hide
and secretly whisper to me
with fluttering wings how you love me

Warm and kind is our friendship
so rare like a beautiful butterfly

Welcome to my garden of happy thoughts
where butterflies fly along
the paths of lovely flowers.

You are so special in my life.
So innocent and pure is our friendship.
I care for you with a heart full of joy.
You are mine, and I love you.

God, help me not to be possessive.
Love is freedom, possession is selfish
God, help me not to be possessive.

(Poet's Note :- When we fall in love, we think love is possessing the other. It takes
time to realize that real love is freedom and never possessive. In every love affair,
God is at play. If not, it is doomed to fail).

MIND IS A PIECE OF PAPER

A plain white piece of paper
is my mind today

It is empty
Like the sky
Empty

During moments of my prayer
the angel of God
scribbles on my mind

words of love, care
forgiveness and beauty

Come scribble on my mind

The word of God

HEAVEN IS NOT A PLACE

Heaven is not a place
But it is a happening
It happens in you and me
In moments of true love.

The inner beauty
and the serenity
in moments of true love
are its own reward.

Heaven happens in selfless love
It has no boundaries, no borders
No distinctions, no denominations
Heaven transcends all religions
And heaven is a monopoly of none

For heaven is not a place
But is a thoughtless thought
That comes to thoughtless clergy
To pacify thoughtless people
When in their misery they suffer.

"You will go to heaven" they say
"Because you believe in Jesus
and in his virgin mother Mary
and in his literal Father, God
Who lives in Heaven eternally
But came to this rotten earth once
Because he loved Mary so dearly."

And indeed I do so believe
For heaven is not a place
But a most glorious thought.

TEACH NOT BIRDS TO SWIM

Teach not a flying bird to swim
Ask not a bird to burrow
It will break its wings and beak.

Force not the eagle
to swim like a fish
Its world is the sky.

Teach not a bird to climb
A monkey can do much better.

Train not the rabbit to fly
Ask not the snake to walk straight.

Teach not the dog to sing
Ask not the squirrel to bark.

Let the peacock dance
Ask not the hen to waltz

Train not the monkey to sing.
Nightingale will croon it for you.

O Teachers, O Educators
If only you knew
The creative potentials
Of the little humans
Entrusted to you !!!

(Poet's Note :- Our schools and universities fail to understand the special creative capabilities of our students. We have to create a positive atmosphere and believe that each and every student entrusted to us is a unique being. Our children have greatness in them and very special talents. Parents should begin it in the family and teachers and professors should continue to challenge and provoke them to get the best out of their uniqueness. It is our sublime duty to the younger generation).

MOTHER CAME IN A CHARIOT

It was a glorious sunset
with waves playing on my feet
gold, red, yellow and amber
as I watched those rays
sucked me in delicate passion.

Their chariot of flames
flew down to me
flames around, all around
golden blue and red
with gleaming eyes I saw

Seven white winged horses
flew into my presence at the shore.

I saw my mummy in the chariot,
smiling like the morning sun.

My eyes opened as sunflowers do
with moonlit eyes
pouring out her blooms of bliss
she whispered to me softly

In joy immeasurable
her voice melted
in hugs and kisses
she murmured in my little ears
'You are my treasure, the apple of my eye'.

She adorned me with the stars,
blessed me with tenderness,
filled me with treasures divine.

I was blissful,
serene and desireless

Singing a glorious hymn
pouring on me her sweetest perfume,
she touched my life from the chariot.

The chariot flew away.

Every dusk,
and every night,
I look at the stars
and murmur:
O twinkling stars!
send my mummy again to me.

I sleep.
Tear drops linger on my lashes.

(Poet's Note :- It is a pleasant vision of my dearest Ma (in Hindi language we call mother so lovingly Maaaaaa). I lost her when i was in the school. She had cancer and died at the age of 38. I yearn for her presence even now every day. It is a great loss i suffered and i will not be cured from the wounds that is created by her absence. When I see the sunset my heart raises itself to her chariot).

Editor's Note :- Hemangi Sharma was not bereaved of her mother at the time of writing this poem. She composed it in September 2010. Here the poet Antony clearly admits that her mother tongue was Hindi. Hence he was an Indian and not German.

SPRING OF MY SOUL

There is a spring in me
that brims and ripples
in the depth of my night.

There is a spring in me
that loves the silence of my heart.

It rushes forth to fill
the valley of my soul
breaking my silence
and then washes me pure

There is a spring in me
in which angels and saints
of heaven come down to bathe
in the silence of my night

At dawn when heavens open
my eyes burst open
like lotus in the pond
when the soft warm rays
kiss its petals open
in joyful wonder of birth

There is a spring in me
in which birds of heaven
fly down to drink
The fluttering of their wings
create music in me
with their splashing and splattering

I love to bathe in the spring of my soul
There is a spring in me that ripples and brims.

(Poet's Note :- I began to bathe in the spring water that welled up in the depths of
my silence at night, and remained there until dawn that purified me.)

THE ANGEL WITHIN

On scraps of raw petals
I poured out verses of love
for the angel in me to sing

The stars twinkled
As moon blinked
in ethereal blues
and myriad colours

The angel in white gown
with flowing sleeves
and a golden crown
began to dance
to the lilting tunes
of my love lined verses.

Like an adoring pilgrim
with love filled eyes
I lifted up my palms
filled with milk of purity

and poured it on your face
like a pure torrent of bliss
the milk flowed down endlessly
onto your eyes, nose, lips, chin
all along the contours of your body.

It was a venerable adoration
beyond any reasoning
no thought no guile
only pure flow of emotion

In the pouring light

of soft morning sun
white clouds lay flat
on the lap of blue sky

At dusk
I heard the whispers of mild rain
and felt the gentle cool breeze
blowing all over me

Fill my heart O Angel
with the gentle music of a flute
touch my lips with a white feather
and make my words mute

Paint my eyelids gold
with the golden rays of dawn
make me lie on your holy lap
like dew drops clinging
to the blooming roses
in your pond.

(Poet's Note :- My adoration of the angel in me cannot be explained by human
reasoning. In the morning and at dusk I pray "fill my heart O Angel and make me
lie on your holy lap". My verses and the angel's song and dance and my adoration
with the milk of purity are my expressions of a devotion of this inner reality in which
I believe. I believe in an angel in me. Do you also believe??)

ASIFA BANO FORGIVES

Five days later
Asifa's body was found.
After seeing her body:

"She had been tortured.
Her legs were broken"
recalled Naseema,
"Her nails had turned black
there were blue and red marks
on her arms and fingers."

Asifa was confined in a local temple
for several days and given sedatives
that kept her unconscious.
She was raped for days,
tortured and then finally murdered
She was strangled to death
and then hit on the head
twice with a stone

She was a "chirping bird"
who ran like a deer
when they traveled,
she looked after the herd.
"That made her the darling
of the community" they said
She was the centre
of our universe, they said.

My heart cries for her
She is an angel among the purest of angels
in the abode of a God
who is beyond all religions.

(Editor's Note :- Asifa was a Kashmir girl. Although Antony has written about
victims in many different countries, the poems have a predominantly Kashmir
connection. Hemangi Sharma was born in Kashmir.)

RELIGION BE A LOVE AFFAIR

With all the power of my being
I shall bless God's holy name.
My soul, do not forget the gifts of God.

God pardons all your iniquities,
redeems you from destruction,
crowns you with kindness and compassion.

God heals all your sicknesses.
He does not chide you.
He does not deal with you
according to your sins.

God will not remember your sins
Because God is all love
The sinners suffer on their own
In the hells they themselves create
Because forgetful of God
They remember their own sins

From morning's first light
to evening's last star
always remember
how special you are
because God thinks of you.

Let your religion be
Less of a dogma
Less of a teaching
And more of a love affair
For loved you are.

NIGHTINGALE'S FEATHERS

I went in search of nightingale feathers
Collected a few from nightingale's nest
And I kept those feathers near my bed
Before I went to sleep

At night i dreamt the nightingale feathers
and they began to sing soft loving melodies

It was such a sweet lullaby
which angels alone can sing
happiness entered
my inner recesses

i went to the feathers and asked
"Wherefrom dear flow
such wonderful melodies
into your hearts' core?"

The feathers told me:
We have the songs in our beaks
We have the songs in our hearts
We have the songs in our brain
we have the songs in our wings

To sing and to sing and to sing
is our benevolent vocation
We sing to the melodies
Of heavenly inspiration
And that is our life
Joy rings out in our souls

This alone is our divine call
We love to live our divine call.

O NIGHTINGALE

O Nightingale, dear Nightingale
Will you be my nightingale
For a night?
At the end of this night
I want to be reborn
As a little nightingale
In your garden of light

Please sing to me
Songs of your soul
I know you are there
I know you are here
Bring me peace
Bring me joy
Sing me to sleep
With your sweetest song

Sing to me
From my heart's core
In your garden of light
Let me soar.

I AM YOUR HIDING ANGEL

I am your hiding angel
May i stay in your heart
as an angel undercover
I am your hiding angel.
No one knows I am here

When you cry I will feel your pain
When it is dark in your heart
I shall bring little twinkling stars

When tears flow down your cheek
I will come unseen to wipe your tears

I shall invite the nightingales
to sing and make you happy
I shall sing in your ears
my sweetest lullaby
when nightingales sleep
I shall sing

And when you are asleep
I shall kiss your sweet lips
until you dream of flowers
birds, skies and heavenly beings

I am the angel of harmony
I want to hide inside you.

(Poet's Note :- This was published in Poetfreak under the name of Genova Maa.
Genova was my beloved mother. She died at the young age of 38. I want to keep
her name alive as long as I am alive).

Editor's Note :- Antony Theodore (Hemangi Sharma) did not have a physical
mother named Genova. Both her parents were alive, both sixty plus, at the time of
publication of this poem. Poet may be referring to Genova In a symbolic manner.

IF YOU LIFT YOURSELF UPTO ME

If you lift yourself up to me
If you lift yourself with all your heart
I shall be with you in your hour of distress
For you have heard the words of my mouth

I shall clothe you with my robe of mercy
I shall gird you with my boundless joy
I shall fix you like a peg in a sure spot
I shall give you honor wherever you are

O God, O unseen God!
Worshiping you in my secret temple
I offer you the incense of love
Before your golden shrine

I shall sing your praises
Playing on the strings
Of my lone Veena
Until you come
And lift me

Will you be pleased
If I dance thus in joy
Through the night
In your holy presence
Until the dawn breaks
Into mild golden rays.

(Poet's Note :- Veena is an Indian musical instrument)

Editor's Note :- Reference to veena shows Antony's Indian roots. Hemangi Sharma
was born in Kashmir as an Indian citizen

SILENTLY I AWAIT

He gently touched me
With his caring hands
There was a spark in my heart
In his eyes there was a glow
Which fired my soul
And I was filled with fire.

Now I get untiring wings
Whenever I think of his love
I can fly across mountains
With the power of that love

I have glided through life
Powered by that love
Across valleys and glades
Over forests and ditches
Undaunted, protected
By that one love.

Now I sit motionless
At the dusk of my life
And think over and over
How great his love was
How great was that love.

Silently I await
For him to appear
In me, some day
Deep down in my soul.

RING NOW THE BELLS

The bird sings
morning light pours in
wake up my little one
time of lullaby is gone

Take your rose
in your little hand
walk in the path of light
leading to the never ending light

Seek for a place
where you can store up
the secrets of your soul
of joy and pain

Come and ring the bells
that sound into the depths of your soul
where you can hear the call
of the one whom your heart loves

The one whom your heart loves.

MY TEARS IN A SHELL

I took my coconut shell
and placed inside it
a thin plastic sheet

At the midnight hours
as the whole world slept
I sat before my earthen oil lamp
shedding tears of suffering and pain
I collected my tears with care

Early before the dawn broke
into thin rays of smiling light
I went to the throne of God
the God of no religion
the God above all religions

Before God's glorious throne
I lifted my shell of tears
in my wounded palms

God looked at me
God saw the wounds of my hands
God saw my ragged clothes

There was only silence,
deep silence that pierced
the heart of heaven

In the silence I saw
tears falling
from God's eyes.

God's tears in my coconut shell.

PURIFY ME, LORD

Purify me, Lord
My life is an open book
Lying before you
Wash me more and more
Every night and day
I cannot hide my sins from you

Touch and purify my heart
My offering today shall be
my contrite heart
you shall not cast away
a contrite heart

Do not turn away from me
wash me in your mercy
and take me to you

I want to be in your presence
at dawn and dusk.
I would like to sit before you
and muse about your wonders

I will delight in your plans for me
unawares you come to me
to plan for me.

When I know of it
my heart is full of joy
who am I Lord
that you think of me?

I know when I cannot pray in words
You hear them all the same
You hear them rising like incense
From the depths of my heart.

TAKE IT FROM ME

Like splendor of the firmament
poor should rise from the dust of earth
those who help the poor and needy
shall be like the stars of heaven

O God here is my
Allotted portion and cup
You it is who gave to me
Take it all from me
Give to the needy and poor

Give them. Let them eat
Let them make merry
And let them enjoy
Life and all its glories

Lord you are the God
Of the needy and the poor
Take my portion and my cup
And give it to the poor

Then show me your path to love
Show me your hand of mercy
Grant me the fullness of joy
In your divine presence
And eternal bliss.

I AM YOUR LOVING MOTHER

I am your mother, loving and holy
Come and suckle from my breasts
until you are no more thirsty
From these consoling breasts
you can always savour with delight

Mine are glorious breasts
You are my beloved one
my child born in intimate love
To whom shall I offer my breasts
if not for you always and ever more

Like a son comforted by his mother
shall I comfort you.
Like a daughter of her heart
I will caress you in love.

At my sight your heart will rejoice
Your bones will flourish like the grass

*****   *****   *****

From my mother flows love and peace
like a river and like a stream in torrents

On her breast alone shall I sleep
Like the nursing infant
I will be fondled in her lap.

Reveal to me O Mother
Reveal yourself to me
Reveal your love, reveal your bounties

when I kneel in prayer
before you
Reveal.

BARTIMEUS CRIED

Bartimeus cried:
Jesus, have pity on me.

Jesus stopped and said:
'call him here'.

Get up, he is calling you.

So throwing off his cloak,
he jumped up and went to Jesus.

'What do you want me to do for you?'
Rabbuni, please, i want to see again.

'Go, your faith has saved you'.
Immediately his sight returned
and he followed him along the road.

Give me the faith of Bartimeus
my Lord and dear God,
the curer of the blind.

YOU ARE MY HIDING PLACE

You are my hiding place
You are my secret cave

There i light my oil lamp
night after night after night

I sit in meditation
I cogitate on your wonders
and on my beads i recite
a million times
about your love that flows
like oil into my lowly heart

I prostate here in my secret cave
adoring you the whole night

You are my hiding place
where I seek my love
night after night.

FASTING ON LENT

Almsgiving and prayer
and fasting shall purify me

It is a time of self-denial,
time of fasting and abstaining
It is a time of prayer in intensity

Deny your body
To rouse the soul
Increase your prayer
So you learn to live
In the light of Lord

It is the primacy of charity and love
over narrow selfish desires
It is the primacy of common good
over the little individual good.

This is the season of
opening up our actions
to a greater expanse
of universal love.

(Editor's Note :- Season of Lent is the name of the fasting season in churches)

DID THE STARS STOP

Did the stars stop twinkling?
Did the moon stop kissing the skies?

Do not lose yourself in despair
Look at the birth of the dawn

The sun rises with its rays
like the peacock spreading
its feathers to dance in the light

After the dusk, there is midnight
The moon will come again to kiss
the skies and the stars will again twinkle

Do not lose hope
Live always in hope
After a dark night
Sun will emerge from sleep.

FIG TREE OF LOVE

The fig tree that God planted
wanted to bear fruits in plenty

But it could not and was sad

In the midst of the night
all alone, it stood and prayed:
Lord God, you who planted me,
I want to give you lots of fruits
But my branches do not produce
fruits that you would like to eat

Would you help me to be fruitful?

Please cultivate the ground around me
Please fertilize me and give me water

I am ready to produce as many fruits
as you would like to have from me.

It is my joy to be fruitful for you
and for all those who come to me.

Make me fruitful O Lord
Of heaven and earth
Make me fruitful for the world.

AND JESUS SPOKE

He was there
where the people fought
and suffered
He was there
where the people refused
to give up hope
He was there
where the poor, disenfranchised
and those who were abandoned
by the rich met.

He was in the midst
of strangers and enemies.

He was in the midst
of laymen and kings

He suffered from the lie
He suffered from falsity

But he stayed true
and saw in his love
the proof of faith

And he spoke words
that his friends and enemies
could not forget.

JOHN THE BAPTIST

John the Baptist
came as a witness
to testify about the light.

"I am the voice of one crying
in the wilderness,
'make straight the way of the Lord'."

Saint John shouted:

"Behold the Lamb of God!",
for Jesus is also the Lamb
that sits upon the throne
and who has authority to open
the seven seals of Revelation.

John the Baptist
should be called more correctly
John the Witness.

Filled with the Holy Spirit
while still in the womb,
he lived for God.

He was the forerunner
of Jesus the Christ.

He had the spirit
and power of Elijah.

Through repentance
and forgiveness of sins
all are called to return
to God Most High.

(Poet's Note :- Reference to the Holy Bible).

ANNOINTED MESSIAH

John identified Jesus
as the anointed Messiah
who is equal with the Father

He proclaimed Him
To be the eternal One
who came after him
and yet existed before him.

And Jesus he identified
as the One sent from heaven
to dispel darkness
as heavenly Lord
of Eternal Life

John knew he was not worthy
to even carry the sandals
of the One about Whom he testified

When we consider the many ways
John bore witness of Christ,
we understand why he said
"He must increase,
but I must decrease"

John did receive great acclaim
as God's prophet,
after 400 years of prophetic silence,
But he was under no illusion
that Jesus must become
increasingly important
while he was to become
of less and less significance.

MARY MEETS ELIZABETH

She came to meet her cousin Elizabeth
Maria the virgin, mother of Jesus Christ
They met, they held hands, and they smiled.
They talked looking into eyes of each other
They touched and conveyed the deepest love
And the respect they had for one another.

Their stomachs touched each other
John and Jesus met already then in womb
And John was taken up by joy in the womb
They smiled, they knew, they prayed
And they submitted to the will of God.

They became the great mothers
of a Prophet and a Messiah himself.
They changed history and culture
They influence humanity even now.
And they will influence human history
Till the end of time
Till the last soul on earth craves love.

(Poet's Note :- In the holy Bible, in the New Testament, this meeting of Elizabeth and Mary is described).

JOSEPH'S DREAM

I became son of Mary
Not of Joseph carpenter
Lord God was my father
But this story of Joseph
I can well imagine now
how it must have fought
and rumbled around in him.

First of all this enigma
his male sense of honor
and a lingering suspicion
that another man it was
who had this something
done with his future wife
that she became pregnant
without his knowledge.

Then the angel came
in the stealth of night
when he was half asleep
half-awake in a dream
and spoke to him
the child was not man's
but from the Holy Spirit.

Look, nothing is impossible for Lord Almighty.
Jesus Christ is of divine origin. Doubt not, believe.
This is the story of Christmas. Rejoice therefore and sing

For in your dream
love speaks
And in a dream
Joseph opens up

In such silent dreams
you hear and see
for dictation of thoughts
is then turned off
and door of the heart
is left unguarded
for divine light to enter

God can then speak
directly to you,
answering your prayers
and addressing things
you would otherwise suppress
or try to regulate
rather too quickly
with your chirping mind.

(Poet's Note :- In the Holy Bible, the story of Joseph' dream is pictured in the holy
Gospel of St. Mathew.)

JESUS LOVE

Jesus spent most of His time
demonstrating this

that the outcasts
and oppressed
matter: the poor

the lepers,
the Samaritans,
the women,
the fishermen,
the orphans,
the widows

also matter

We shall also
demonstrate
what Jesus did

We should aim
to live like Christ

and spend more
and more of our time
demonstrating that

Hispanic lives matter
Jewish lives matter
Muslim lives matter
Native American
lives matter

Immigrant lives matter
Asian lives matter
and Black lives matter.

CHRISTMAS BELLS ARE RINGING

Listen O birds and animals
Trees and flowers and leaves
Rivers and seas everywhere.
The Christmas Bells are ringing.

The old and familiar singing
on the streets this cold evening
They are sweet and they bring
our sweet childhood memories
when we sang with mummy dearest
lovely songs of love and mercy
and a new birth of Jesus Christ.

Now think of the millions of abortions
and the killing of innocent children
the abandoned and the homeless
the forced child labor of little ones
silently killing their lovely future
no smile, no school
no play, no joy
entire spring of their lives spent
toiling for the mighty and the rich.

Human beings, sing with the angels
"Let there be peace on this earth
and glory to God in the mighty heavens
Be of goodwill, spread smiles everywhere".

The belfries of all Christendom
ring out in an unbroken song:
"peace, peace, joy, joy everywhere
goodwill, goodwill for all men".

Let us sing together:
Sing it on our way, at dawn and dusk,
sublime chanting and dancing along
"peace on earth, for men
and for good willed women!"

ISIS is killing, Taliban is killing
Terrorists are killing
In the name of God
In the name of religion
Beheading the innocent
Cutting their throats slowly
With a small knife, slowly
Giving them a slow, painful death
because Christ's name is on their lips.

Let all religions unite.
"We shall not kill in the name of God".

Bow your head and heart
and chant in your heart
"We shall not hate
We shall only love
And we shall spread
God's joy and peace"

The pealing of bells from the towers
I can hear loud, clear and deep.

God is not dead
God is not asleep
Peace shall prevail
Goodwill in the hearts
Of men and women
Shall reign till the end of times.

PART – II

WORD OF GOD

SOUNDS FROM ETERNITY

TALKING WITH GOD

God knows the thoughts of our hearts before they land on our tongues. One who tunes into God knows the thoughts welling up in all human hearts. One who loves God knows how to talk to God in silence.

For wherever life is, there is talking. Talking is a beauty of life link, of being in existence. Talk of feelings, talk of emotions, talk of not only words but heavenly responses to nature, wind, breeze, ocean, sky, birds and all. In silence body talks, in darkness inner light talks. At night the nocturnals talk. In peace hearts talk with love. In harmony music talks with symphonies. Talking without words is the most beautiful talking. Talking with dance, talking with lyrics, talking with memories, nostalgic. When you are old and alone, you will talk to photos of dead ones, to tombs of dead ones, to your beloved ones gone by. You talk to your own feelings, you talk to them who are in your consciousness. Talking is as enormous as your silent gifts of love.

Talk to God. Talk with your heart absorbed in God. Listen incessantly to God's silent talk. Do not underestimate the power of the Word. And do not forget that the pen is mightier than all the injustices that holy earth can contain. Writing is a source of personal soul-searching to find the meaning of life on earth.

SAINT BERNHARD'S CONFESSION

I confess, then O man
Though I say it in my foolishness
That the Word has visited me
And even very often so

But though He has entered
Frequently into my soul
I have never at any time sensed
The precise moment of His coming

I have felt He was present
I remember He has been with me
I have even had presentiment
That He would come to me
But I was never able to feel
His coming nor His departure

Whence He came to enter my soul
Or whither He went on quitting it
And by what means He made
His entrances or departures
I confess that I know not
Even to this day.

(Poet's Note :- Reference to St. Bernard, "Cantica Canticorum ", Sermon lxxiv) .

DANTE'S VISION

And I believe that I saw
the universal form
of this complexity
and yet simplicity
because, as I say this
I feel I rejoice more deeply

Oh, but how scant it was
the speech that ensued
and how faint to my concept !
and that to what I saw is such
that it suffices not to call it 'little'

O Light Eternal
Who only in Thyself abidest,
only Thyself dost comprehend,
and, of Thyself comprehended
and Thyself comprehending,
dost love and smile! "

(Poet's Note :- Taken from Dante, Divine Comedy, Paradise, xxxiii.82ff, & 121ff) .

ARK OF ACACIA

Have them make an ark
of gentle acacia wood
two and a half cubits long
a cubit and a half wide
a cubit and a half high

Overlay it with pure gold
inside and out
make a gold molding
all around

Cast four gold rings
fasten them to the four feet
two rings on one side
two rings on the other

Then make poles
of acacia wood
overlay them with gold

Insert the poles
into the gold rings
on the sides of the ark
to carry it

Poles are to remain
in the rings of the ark
Remove them not

Put in the ark
tablets of the covenant
which I will give
unto you.

(Poet's Note :- Reference to Exodus 25,10-16 of the Holy Bible)

WORD OF GOD

Read the word of God
love God's word
and value it more
than your daily bread.

For man shall not live
By bread alone
But by every word
That comes from God
Listen intently therefore
to the Word of God
read out aloud.

Reflect on its glory
hour by hour
with every passing day
Meditate upon it
morning by morning
and store it up
within your heart
at close of each day

Then alone will you know
power of the Word
the Word of God
is a living truth
which abides in you
forever and ever.

FIRE IS HIS HEAD

Fire is His head,
the sun and moon
are His eyes
space His ears,
the Vedas His speech
the wind His breath
the universe His heart

From His feet the Earth
has originated
Verily, He is
The innermost self

of all beings.

(Poet's Note : Inspired by The Upanishads.)

Editor's Note :- God is addressed as Agni or "Fire" in most of the Vedic mantras.)

BREAD OF LIFE

I am the Living Water
I am the bread of life
I am the breath of life
I am the light of the world.

We need water
We need bread
We need Atem of life.
We need light.

Jesus Christ promises
all that we need in life

How can anyone
ever deny God?

Sleep in hope
Sleep in peace
Sleep in grace

Every night
go to bed
with God
and the angels.

Sleep in peace
my friends always

This is faith.

Editor's Note :- Man shall not live on bread alone, but on every word that comes
out of the mouth of God (Mathew 4.4)

OM AND AMEN

Those in whose hearts
the Word reverberates
as OM unceasingly
are indeed blessed
and deeply loved
as one who is the Self.

The all-knowing Self
was never born
nor will it die.

Beyond cause and effect,
This Self is eternal
and immutable.

When the body dies,
the Self does not die.

The whole mantra AUM
beginningless, endless
indivisible, unbroken
goes on reverberating in the mind.

Established in this cosmic vibration,

the sage goes beyond
fear, decay, and death
to enter infinite peace
Amen. Amen. Amen.

(Poet's Note :- From the Katha and Prashna Upanishad, great Hindu Scriptures)

YOU ARE INFINITE

O Almighty!
You are the infinite;
the universe is also infinite!

From the infinite
the infinite has come out!

Having taken infinite
out of the infinite,
the infinite alone remains!

O Almighty!
May there be Peace!
Peace everywhere
Peace!

(Poet's Note :- From the Ishavashya Upanishad, the great Hindu Scripture)

MAKE ME WATER, LORD

Lord I wish to be like water
that carries ships and boats
on its way to human beings
in the nooks and corners
of your villages and cities.

I want to bring goods to the poor

I want to make the roots of trees wet
I want to help the trees to carry fruits
that the poor on the banks may pluck
and eat filling their poor stomachs.

I want to live for the poor to feed them,
educate them, clothe them, love them.

Lord make me like the humble water
help me to flow and reach to the poor.

Give me little waves that will smile
when I touch the feet of the poor.

Lord make me like humble water
carrying promises of your word
to quench the thirst of the poor.

(Editor's Note :- The Word of God was heard by many Christian saints as the sound
of many waters.)

PRAYER IS MY INCENSE

LORD, I call out to you
come quickly to me.

Hear my voice
when I call to you.

May my prayer be
set before you like incense;
may the lifting up
of my hands be like
the evening sacrifice.

Set a guard over my mouth,
O Lord; keep watch
over the door of my lips.

(Poet's Note :- Refer Holy Bible. Psalm 141:1)

IDEA OF GOD

All creatures below man
correspond to the pattern
God has in His Mind.

A horse is a horse
because it gallops
to God's idea
of a horse's gallop.

A tree is truly a tree
because it corresponds
to God's idea
of growth in a tree.

A rose is a rose
because it is
God's idea
of a rose
wrapped up
in chemicals
and tints and life.

THE RICH YOUNG MAN

Jesus' conversation
with the rich young man
continues till today
in every period of history
including our own.

What good must I do
to enter eternal life?
This is the question
that arises in the heart
of every individual,
and Christ alone can answer
the full and definitive answer

Jesus tells the young man:
If you would enter life,
keep the commandments.

And the young man says
I have followed the commandments
Whereupon Christ tells him
Sell all that you have
Distribute them to the poor
And then follow me
If you shall have life eternal.

Christ begins with commandments
because they are the condition
the basic manifestation of love
For neighbor and for God.

DAVID THE SHEPHERD

David was after God's heart
and he spent all his hours
reflecting on the blessings
he received from God

From early years
when he tended his father's flock
till his dying days
as the shepherd king of Israel
David was a man tested
who proved that the Lord
was a faithful God
Whose Word
as the sages had heard
was to be trusted.

For him the Lord was a God
Who kept His promises
Whose loving kindness
and great goodness
never failed.

"The Lord is my Shepherd,
I shall not want for myself..."

David wrote
as he meditated
day and night
on the Word

God restores me
my faith
my soul.

SPIRIT HUG

I am sending you
a Spiritual Hug

It will lift you
nourish you
in your darkest hour

I just want you to know
that God loves you
and you are not alone
in your battle
God is with you

Put your faith in Him
keep moving forward
feel motivated
for better days
are yet to come

God will bless you
because you are
cute and adorable

Dream high
Work hard
Never be idle
Live with a purpose

You will live
in abundance
Life will reward you
every tear that you shed

every trouble that you tread
will be rewarded duly
with greater happiness.

Never give up
have faith in the Word
if doubts creep in
remember the Word

all the answers
to the questions you ask
are within you

imbedded
in deep faith.

GOD BREATHED

God breathed
and stars appeared
in the firmament.

It was a glorious scene.

God was very happy
to see the stars born
out of God's breath.

Then God collected
waves of the ocean
and stored them up
in caves of the sea
in those depths.

Revere Him
He is the Lord of
the universe.

He is love eternal.

(Editor's Note :- According to Upanishads, the holy scriptures glorifying the Word
of God are the breath of the Eternal)

ARE YOU LISTENING?

Lord God
I am constantly talking to you
Listen to my word

Do you really listen to me?
Sometimes i doubt it
Sorry for being like this

But I am a simple human being
I like to converse with you like this

You like me more when i am simple
and when i am very open to you.
Is it not?

Help me to call on your holy name
Help me to make sense of your Word
before I turn to ask for help
from people here on earth

Look !!!
i am constantly conversing with you

Word for Word
Lost in the Word

YOU ARE WORTHY

You are worthy
You are powerful
You are unique
You are strong
You are special
You can choose
how to react to life

Life doesn't happen
to you. Life happens for you.

Let go of all resistance
Be grateful for everything
that you have in life
do not focus on things
that you do not have.

You are living right now
Life is too short to worry
about what you do not have.

Live life and prosper
Nothing is impossible
Do not be crazy
Be yourself

Do not care about
what others think

If you let that affect you,
you will never be happy.

PART – III

MYSTERY OF LOVE

MAN AND THE OTHER HALF

LOVE ALONE

The whole life is a search for a little bit of love. If we do not get it, we become psychologically and physically ill. If we experience it, then there is Rhythm in our souls and we dance in those rhythms...

All the moments in which you do not love, are wasted moments of life which will never come back. Our call is to love. There is no meaning in life without love.

Love and love alone can bring you into the world of beauty. Your soul is in need of love. The deepest longing in you is love. Love is spiritual nourishment.

Love is God's hands and arms. He hugs his beings through love. When we are pure in mind, or when there is no mind, God puts his hand made of divine energy through our hearts. Through us that hand goes to the heart of our beloved. Now who are you, and who am I, to stop, start, punctuate, and intervene that love?

COME WITH ME, ELOPE

Come we shall swim
This ocean of love
Have no fear now
I am with you always
Don't you see?

Come, we shall swim away
and elope together
to the other shore
when we reach that shore
I shall help you climb
on rainbows with me

We shall be in light
clad in colors of joy
in smiles, in peace
we shall then kiss
and thousands of angels
will be looking at us
in wonderment

Do you elope
with me now
my love?

SUN KISSED

The tropical sun kisses me
on both my cheeks today
as I go talking and chatting
to the flitting butterflies
on the way to my school

I feel the warmth and the cold
of dark skinned forest leaves
I hear the music of the leaves
when wind blows on them

I imagine they are all lovers,
the trees, the leaves and the wind
and I want to be the wind

flying along the shuffling leaves
and making them dance
to the undulating tunes
of my whistling breeze
and making them smile

softly with me.

CRUSH ME AND POSSESS ME

Allow me to be the clay
in your powerful hands

Play on me my Lord
Like a master player
Beat me down as you like
to shape me as you will

I shall become what
you want me to be

Only then I shall find
real and eternal joy

Beat me down
and crush me
possess me.

STIR MY NOOKS AND CRANNIES

O eternal flame of love,
how I wait that you kindle in me
your fire of love?

Would you blaze down
my selfish seeking
to soothingly wound me again
till you reach the roots of my soul

Touch me in my depths
in my crannies
with the soft touch
of your Love

Destroy this superficial display
of naked affluence
and lead me
to freedom
of selflessness.

Stir in my nooks and crannies
the desire for true love
and help me lie awake
till morning hours
in your loving presence.

MELODY OF YOUR FLUTE

O sweetheart
melodies of your flute
have stolen my heart

When your celestial tunes
reached my ears
I lost consciousness
I felt i lost my body

Was i in a trance??

I saw my God
sitting by my side
playing melodious Ragas
of sweet romance

And lying on my bed
i was mesmerized
and transfixed.

DANCER BECOMES THE DANCE

Forget the dancer
Kill this ego
Go to core of ego
Become humble
now break the ego

That will be the first step
and then you can dance
you can become the dance

Dancer becomes the dance
call it prayer or meditation
call it zen or contemplation

Call it whatever
by whatever name
whatever it is

When you dance without knowing
who it is dancing
then alone you dance
The dancer becomes the dance.

AND THE MOON SMILED

In tiptoeing tiny steps
I came to you
to pluck your soul

You found me, hugged me
then kissed me
and squeezed my lips

like this

And then…
plucked your soul to give me
and then the moon smiled.

(Poet's Note :- True love experience is always a mystery. "The smile of the moon"
- the mild golden light of the moon that falls in the garden on the riverbanks was
always mysterious for me.)

SECRET HUGS

The roots of the earth
hug and kiss secretly
in their dark chambers
and the sand is happy to see
those secret hugs and kisses

Desire for secret romance
wells up in their hearts
and the sand around the roots
begins to hug earnestly
along their hidden widths
and secret lengths

They are busy now
hugging and kissing
in a royal romance

The poet saw it,
was tickled and smiled.

RISK OF LOVE

Take the risk
to love

It is worth
taking it

Love is life
Life is love

I wish you
a dream of love

I acknowledge my sins
I did not cover up my guilt
When I opened up to God

I confessed my fault to the Lord
and God washed away
the guilt of my sins.

My soul is white
like the morning snow that falls
from the glory of heavens

Love was the risk
I took on my path to God
And God rewarded me

with love.

LET LOVE BLOOM

I send unconditional love
and light to you

May God send to you
the highest energies
of healing, restoration
and regeneration
in you.

may the flowers bloom
trunks heal
leaves spread
seeds sprout

May the souls of all beings
all the innocent animals
birds, insects and fish
the people, and nature
that have died in the wildfire
rest in heavenly peace

let love bloom.

(Poet's Note :- Written after reading about the wild forest fire.)

WE WERE A SINGLE MELODY

You and I,
we sang like little nightingales
You sang, I sang
We were a single melody

We shared sweet smiles,
You were the lips, I was the smile

In times of tears
You held me close to you
You wiped my tears
I held your hand

You were the flesh, I was the skin

The golden sun smiled,
you were the gold, I was the light

You hugged me, I caressed you
You were the fingers, I was the body

When the songbird sang in our hearts
You were one wing, I was the other wing

We were two candles but one flame

I was the sparkling sea,
You were the ripples

You sing, I sing
We are a single melody.

STARLIT NIGHT BY RIVULET

On a starlight night
all alone I sat
on a small rock
near the rivulet
that was flowing peacefully
near the paddy fields

Looking into the sky
I saw the little white stars
twinkling like loose petals
on a warm nuptial bed
And then I looked around
at dark fields stretching
to horizon and beyond
solitude engulfed me
in its vast blackness

How i wish to be a star
on the black firmament
How i wish to emanate
light in this dark world.

MY HEART IS TORN

My heart is torn, oh torn
Where is my lovely moon today?
Where is the light falling on the flowing river?
Where are all the melodies of the flute
which the shepherd used to play?
Where is the child which smiled all the way?
Where is the rose?
did it lose its colour today?
I hear only mourning women
Did anybody die in the village?
Why is it so gloomy all around
when the sun is shining still?

My heart is torn, oh torn
My beloved, my heart is torn

I need the oil of gladness
Who will pour it into my grieving soul?

O God will you command an angel
to fly down into my valley of misery
to embalm me with the oil of love?

I am so lonely, lonely
I have no one in this busy world
so lonely, lonely

O come, O come heavenly beings,
hug me, kiss me, hold me
caress me, care for me
O someone

For my heart is torn, torn.

RINGING THE BELLS OF LOVE

Early this morning
in your temple where you live
I stand before your holy shrine
ringing the bells of love

Would you come down from your holy shrine
my lover of my heart to look at me
I need only your eyes to see me now

I was dying with longing the whole night
sleepless was I on my cozy bed
I did not wink, did not rest

Before the morning cock crew
I came to you to your holy shrine
to tell you that I love you
That I love you, love you
more than anyone else in this world

I die with longing for your presence
I need only your eyes to see me now.

MY FLESH PINES FOR YOU

My soul thirsts for my god
My flesh pines for you
Don't you see
How I pine, pine?

Allow me to gaze upon you
In your holy sanctuary
Have mercy on me
My dear Beloved!

Cast me not away
Make me your own
Give me a little place
In the great expanse
Of your beautiful heart

My lips shall glorify you
They will sing of you
With exultant lips
My mouth shall praise you.

LOVE IN THE REDWOODS

I walked slowly
through the redwoods
where the trees
talk with God

I murmured to the trees
leaning on them

They took my heart
and my thoughts
and turned them into songs

The redwoods sang
those songs in tunes
unheard

It is true
the redwood trees
talk with God.

GOD KNEW I NEED SOMEONE

God knew that I need someone
To keep as a treasure in my heart
Someone who is so true
Fine and caring

God knew that I need smiles
To walk on my hard path
And to dress my wounds
With love

God knew I need the consciousness
Of someone who thinks of me
In the night when the moon shines
And water sleeps in comfort

God knew that I need to share
My joys and my sorrows
With someone who wiped my tears
And caressed my hair so lovingly

God knew that I need a lap
Where I can sleep like a sweet cat
And get up to see the first rays of sun
Which loves to shine in my eyes

God knew and he gave…..

(Poet's Note :- Mixing up of the tenses in this poem is intentional)

Editor's Note :- Hemangi Sharma repeatedly told me that she had been
desperately seeking a soul companion after all her earlier relationships broke
apart in disaster.

IMAGINE THAT LOVE

In the middle of an ordinary life
love gives me a fairytale

If human love is so full of joy
How will it be when i taste the love
of God on the lips of my heart?

Will it be like a thousand
fairy tales of lovers
in intimate moments?

Will it be like the moon
in its world, murmuring,
words of love with the skies?

Will it be like the butterflies
sucking the liquid nectar
from the heart of the flowers
in wild ecstasy?

Will it be like the secret moments
shared by engrossed lovers
on moonlit sandy beaches
where the lovely fairies play
on their harps and then sleep?

How will it be, tell me
O poets of love.

(Poet's Note :- God You Are My God - Psalm 63)

COME, TOUCH ME

Touch me
here, like this

Touch me
to feel the life
within you.

Touch me
Once more
Again and again
Come touch me
Like this

Only when you go out
of your own self

to touch, to feel

only then
will you
know
what is love.

MAY I EMBRACE YOU

May I embrace you first,
A tight and intense embrace
Before we enter into the dance
Of divine love?

You dance with soft steps
And slowly take me to sudden gusts
And I enjoy it like the Lotus
At the first rays of the Sun

Then in a moment of deep love
You look into my waiting eyes
The shine of which
I shall never forget

You cradle my body
Your lips are warm and moist
And my eyes are filled with Joy

I feel your whisper in my ears
My hairs love your fingers now
And your lips begin to dance on me

I forget all that is mundane
And fly to the heavens
To tell my God
'I am now in divine love'.

HAVE I LOVED ENOUGH?

We cannot enter the gates
of eternal life
or even begin to enjoy
life on earth
if we do not love
if we do not love enough

for it is in loving God
and loving our neighbor
that we have a relationship
with God and neighbor

Your friend is your neighbor
The beggar on the street
The prostitute, the leper
The homeless, the friendless
Is your neighbour

But the young man's question
is not yet fully answered

For he then tells Christ
I have kept the commandments
Ever since my youth
What more should I do
To obtain divine favour?

Jesus challenges him further
Son, no half measure at all
Leave behind every obstacle
Go sell everything you have
Give them away to the poor
And then "Come, Follow me"

WILL YOU HUG ME

When the roses wait
for kiss of the dew
when first rays of sun
touch the tiny beaks
of singing love birds
when in my soft smiling lips
and in my shining eyes
you see thousand little stars
hiding in my soul

secretly

would you hug me innocently
and give me a soft kiss
on my aching lips
whose memory will lead me
from this glorious dawn
through to the dusk?

MY SACRED SECRET

Buds are born in me
In deep meditation
My heart sighs for the lord of my soul
And the buds bloom into flowers
Full of fragrance
And sweet love
My soul loves him
More than ever before

I compose a new song for him
Inside my secret little cave
And sing it all alone on my harp
It echoes on the walls of my soul
And I smile in silent bliss
With the golden flame
Of the little lamp of my cave

In the depth of silence
It echoes and re-echoes
Within my soul's walls
This song of love
Which I sing
For him alone
Whom my soul loves

It is my sacred secret
My soul loves him now
More than anyone else.

KISS OF LIFE

When i kiss you
I kiss my own awareness
At your holy presence

You are divine
I am divine
I kiss your divinity
When your lips touch mine

I am lost in you
You are lost in me
And we search each other
Unawares

You find me
I find you
In a moment sublime
In each other

In reverent awareness
I enter silently
and bow
in my cave of
indescribable sweetness.

OUR FIRST KISS

I walked down to the rivulet
near the wild flowers
in our little village

And I sat under the flower tree
on this evening of beatitude
in the mild long sun rays
of the setting sun

Here we kissed for the first time

You are not here now
but still I feel
your mystified presence
everywhere in me

This presence is more than real
I feel your lips on my lips
your chest on my chest
your love spreading down
my whole being

It is more than the real
you are here in ethereal
mystified loving presence

I feel divine at this moment.

I WANT TO KISS

The little stream sings
and dances in great joy
on its way to the flower tree
its waters bubble and froth
when it thinks madly
of the flower tree

I want to flow fast
like the wild stream
and kiss the roots
of my flower tree
my tree will blossom
into plentiful buds
beautiful and new
of every hue

Do you know now
this secret of love
and its little mystery
that brings forth buds
on my flower tree?

I want to flow fast
I can't wait anymore
to kiss the roots
of my lover tree.

LOVE ALONE

I put no trust in my bow
I put no trust in my arrow

my sword does not bring me victory

It is you who give us victory
It is your mighty arm that saves us

In your power and intelligence
you lead us through valleys
and the deserts and hills
to fight against our enemies

We take bold steps and jump up
for you are there with us
in front and at the back
to keep us safe and sound
and bring us back home

in our love cradle.

DAWN SONG

I am a night bird
seeking the first rays
on the horizon
eagerly waiting
for daybreak

As you know
dawn has its songs

Bird of dawn is singing
of my longings

What consolation
for my aching heart
The meadow bird
is flying around me

Her flight pleases
the universal soul
ever present in
everything that exists.

IN THE BUBBLE OF LOVE

To become a single vibration
with one single breath of my Stella
warm and cold, soft and bold
To live and to die each moment
in the arms of my beloved Stella
I want to flow within the pain
and the pleasures of my love
for my umpteenth resurrection.

Love is my greatest vocation
My poetic heart craves for love
Stella is its divine personification

Earth is bubbling to touch my ecstasy
While spirit passes through outward coitus
Heart still struggles to vibrate and imitate
Life's offerings of happiness to ruminate
I think of death, and of love in death
as a place of silent peaceful abode

I was a vain man till I found love
A living sepulcher, an acolyte I became
The mystery of unknown realms
That a tiny flower knows
The knowledge of eternal vastness
That a dew drop knows
The voiceless voice of a bird
That sings fluently of infinity
I had become forgetful of it all.

My feeling of no feeling is now vast in its profundity
My kingdom is empty like a mirror with no image inside
My world shrinks within its womb In an endless wrap

Within me I feel many bodies
a hundred separate existences
each one feels real yet unreal
and I hurtle forward through life
to death in love and dreams

Will this blood of mine redeem the fallen one?
Will this gore that gushed out of my hurt heart
Resurrect those who have fallen from Grace?

I feel crucifixion of the Lord
when I think of my love
and my own crucifixion
Will it save anyone

It blossomed without root
and how chaotic it's become
My mind as wandering bee
is now drawn to somnolence

Where is that old self
That desire to touch
The holiest heights?

Love is not bondage
I begin to know now
Love is liberation itself.

[Poet's Note :- This poem expresses my dear friend Prabir's feelings for his muse
Stella]

MAN, WOMAN, DESIRE

You feel the primordial urge
rising up your spine
as it seeks release
through your extremities
sexual urge is God's design
and it has divine origin
channeling through our lives
in many different ways

our bodies remind us
we are not alone
not meant to be alone
male and female
female and male
the opposites tension
attract and repel

you feel virtue of love
and the guilt of sin
but sexual desire
is not a bad thing

It may lead us to temptation
It may lead us to sin
But sexual union
Is God's own design
He has given us the desire
For intimate union
To remind us we were
Only made for love

man and woman
woman and man

symmetry in asymmetry
each one a complement
and mirror of the other

a man needs a woman
woman needs a man
to complement each other
to attain fullness in body
and oneness in spirit

Our romantic feelings
and sexual longings
compel us not to have sex
just for the sake of sex
but to pursue covenant

the desire invites us
to a lifelong vow
of shared intimacy

We were created by God
not for the shared urge
of a sexual relationship

We were created by God
only for committed love
and intimate knowing.

MARRIAGE SACRAMENT

Sexual intimacy in love
is a divine celebration
of man's covenant with God

Sacred sexual joys
with your spouse
in marriage
is a physical way
of celebrating vows
you make before marriage

Intimacy of sex
within marriage vow
is in some ways
similar to a sacrament

We give away our bodies
as offering to each other
in such a passionate way
and become vulnerable
in complete surrender

mirroring how we have vowed
our entire lives to each other.

COVENANT OF MARRIAGE

This is why sex acts
and sexual intimacy
should be reserved
for holy covenant
of marriage vows

male and female
man and woman
must unite together
under oath of love

sexual betrayal
is a living metaphor
of the spiritual reality
of breaking cruelly
our covenant with God

Sexual fidelity is the promise
of a marriage covenant
greatest call within marriage
is complete faithfulness

Broken vows are a tragedy
creating waves of pain
that greedy world suffers

Sexual intimacy in marriage
symbolizes faith in church
that our intimacy with God
is meant to be passionate
and vulnerable
and it requires surrender
and giving of ourselves.

BETWEEN HUSBAND AND WIFE

The one-flesh intimacy
Between husband and wife
On the altar of love
It is a reflection of Christ
And the church in man

Intimacy is the secret
Of godliness in man
In intimate moments
You see the One
And forget yourself

This forgetfulness
Of your little self
And start of the journey
From self love to god love
Is the goal of marriage

Paul sees the connection
Between marriage and church
Both are for the faithful
Faithless cannot travel
Through to eternal life

And this is a "mystery"
Says Paul
It also means
We cannot yet grasp
The fullness of this metaphor.

WITNESS OF LOVE

When I married my love
we entered covenant
in the sight of God
following the Word
of our Holy Scripture
marriage was a sacrament
in which we made our vows
for life long sharing
and caring together

God is the witness
to our sacred vows
and he holds us to it
if we neglect or break
we break our covenant
with our dearest Lord

A covenant of marriage
is not a piece of paper
not fine sounding words
nor glittering jewelry
nor songs and dance
in a ceremony of show

Marriage is our word
Promised to the Lord
In presence of the world
To make our love known
And so it becomes One
With the Word of God.

ALTAR OF LOVE

I lost myself within you
our souls entwined
our bodies bound
our minds in tune

What remained of me
When I was lost in you?

The words you spoke
came straight from my heart
and i instantly knew
everything about you
is so hauntingly familiar

My heart is captured
On your altar of love
I want to fly away
But no, but no
I know I cannot

Like the sage falling
before the Holy Altar
I have knelt and surrendered
Fully into your hands

Fully.

MY LOVE AND YOURS

With all my love
and yours, love
with all of me
and you together
we shall succeed
in all our dreams
and in all our goals

You have made it, my love
to this equal ness of level
in spiritual frequencies
from which I profit now.

DRY WEEDS OF LOVE

I collected dry weeds
from sun burnt banks
of the bone dead river
in hot summer of life

I brought them home
and watered the weeds
pressed them to my heart
beaming with fresh love

Just a little touch
here and there
and they became
lovely little flowers.

NEAR YOUR GRAVE I STAND

Your love gave me warmth
It made me feel like being me
Your love gave me power

The music in me kept playing
Many lovely romantic songs
We kissed silently in the rain
When no one was watching
And then you hugged me
Suddenly, pulling me up
Pressing me to your chest

Once you made me awake
You drove in the midnight
On the lovely beach road
When all the stars blinked
And sent rays of blessings
On us hugging, caressing
And kissing in the car

How can I ever forget
Those lovely romantic moments
For the more I think of you
The more I feel you in me

***** ***** *****

Now near your grave
I stand alone tonight
With a blooming flower
In my trembling hand

And I look up to the mighty heavens
And pray: keep my lover safe
O mighty God, in your protective hands.

PART – IV

VOYAGE OF LIFE

ACROSS LAND AND THE SEA

Caught between the devil and the deep sea I am dying. Either I suffer from bereavement or drowned and soaked I get wet forever eternally drowned. What to do, I am too much in love that I am burning with love. O Lord, guide me to the other shore...

A poet is the one who keeps plenty of secrets and sometimes spontaneously he begins to sing in his soul and then writes them down. When he forgets himself and writes it becomes a poem which touches and sometimes converts the reader.

Do not first buy, but just be a co-traveler, in the roads of life, in the road to heaven, have a passer-by who shall forever be a companion who needs no explanation for smiling or crying. Have a hand, that knows when to support, have a heart that knows when to throb, have a lip that knows when to kiss or not to. Have a hug that knows when to or not to. Do not buy, but be a fellow good Samaritan. After all life is only a ladder to reach God's paradise.....

A TORTOISE TAUGHT ME

Once I asked a rabbit
You run about so fast
So many places you see
You will have so much
in your mind to tell me
about this world of beauty

But the rabbit could not tell me much

Then I went to the tortoise
"Would you tell me
about this beautiful world? "

The tortoise smiled
opening its mouth slowly
and told me a lot
about this beautiful world

I listened, and listened
and I learned a lot

I see the beauty of nature
now, which I never noticed
in my fast and busy life.

QUO VADIS

Come to my church
by the river Inn
from outside it looks
like a crystal of rock

It is inscribed here
on the wooden door
"Quo Vadis?"
Where are you going?

Where am I going today
Am I going to meet
Lord of the universe
born in the dirt, with cattle
food trough and a manger?

Where am I going
can bring to light
meaning of my life

My life has no other meaning
but for the presence of Almighty
in my thinking and in my heart

And today I am going to meet
Him for crucifixion of my sorrow.

(Poet's Note :- There is a church in Innsbruk, Austria whose exterior resembles a rock crystal. Reference is to the door grille of this church built by Richard Kurt Fischer in Innsbruck-Arzl in 1991).

Editor's Note :- "Divine, Quo Vadis" is Latin version of "Lord where are you going". When St Peter was fleeing from Rome to escape persecsion, he saw Jesus entering the City. When he was asked where he was going, Jesus answered that "I am going to Rome to be crucified again."

I HEARD THE GALLOPING HORSES

I heard the galloping of horses
They were distant sounds
But they came nearer
and nearer to me

And I saw
the galloping horses
came in my direction

I waited anxiously

In a moment without asking me
they entered the cave of my heart
penetrating the closed doors
of my heart, not violently

They galloped and galloped
and travelled inside my cave.

I did not know that i had so much
of space in the cave of my heart

And still I hear
The galloping of horses.

I AM A VAGABOND

God
You are there
I'm here

like the street beggar
I am wandering
like a vagabond

I am
caste-less
creed-less

I am a monk
on the path of love
on the path of life

An humble ascetic life
I lead in this crowded world

I do not know who I am
but I do know and feel
You are very near to me.

(Poet's Note :- Inspired by the comments of Indian poet Mahtab Bangalee)

I WENT TO HIMALAYAS

I went to the foot of Himalayas
I wanted to shake up Himalayas
And you did know my resolve.....
Do you think i am mad?

i shook and shook Himalayas

i realized God is like this
UNSHAKEN
Those who put their lives
and TRUST in God
will never be shaken

This realization made me happy
i smiled like a child today
Do you think i am mad?
But there is a joy
in this madness
Isn't it?

It is.

FROM THE VALLEY I CRIED

From the valley i cried
God heard my cry.

God came to the top of the mount
and called out to me
"come to me".

How shall i come?
I am in the valley.

God disappeared
then i saw to my surprise
an angel flew down to me
in the valley of tears
in my valley of loneliness
to take me away
upon the angel's wings.

We flew and flew and flew
We flew and flew.

A SPARROW IN THE NEST

Like eagles in the cliffs
I slept in the arms of my God

Like sparrows in their nests
I chattered in the presence of my God

Like a wounded dove
I shivered in his presence
And wept bitterly

until I had no tears.

I RAN INTO LIGHT

i entered into a cave
It was very dark in there
i went forward in the darkness
and i entered into a tunnel
In the absence of light in tunnel
i heard voices behind me
in terrible fear i looked back
then i heard footsteps in front
and it went on for some time
then somehow i got the notion
"I am not alone in this tunnel"

It gave me courage
i walked on and on
all alone, but not alone

At the end of the tunnel
i saw light. Light !!
It was so powerful
i could not open my eyes

In the direction of the light
at the end of the tunnel
i ran on, like a joyful deer

It was light and only light

And it was paradise
Abode of "The Almighty",
Who is above all darkness
Who is above all religion

(Poet's Note :- The small i symbolizes that one should become lesser and lesser
as one proceeds to the eternal abode) .

Editor's Note :- It has been Hemangi Sharma's life-long obsession with a small "i".

I CLIMBED UP THE HILL

This morning i love you my God
I love you more than my heart's fill

In the night I climbed up the hill
The rocky way was not hard at all
While I thought of you always uphill

You are my dear Lord and God
My heart's solace is your Word

My heart will not come to peace
Until I reach you my Lord God

This holy morning I reached the top

I call you looking up to the heavens
I raise up my hands to you

Do you listen to me my God?

Come and show me your face
Oh the faceless and body-less one
How shall I ever see your face?.

ACROSS THE PROBLEM OCEAN

When the problem ocean is so great
Then it is really great and big. It is simply so.
But my God is greater than that.

When the fear mountain is so high
Then is it really mighty and high. And that's it.
But my God is mightier than that.

When the sadness desert is so vast
Then it is really wide and vast. You find no end.
But my God is vaster than vast.

God has no beginning
And God has no end
Mightier than the mighty
Higher than the most high
God has simplest solutions
For the toughest problems

When I find it impossible to proceed
God comes to me and tells me
You have cried a lot. It is enough
I shall come to share your suffering
And I shall wash away all your tears.

WALKING ON THE WAVES

Walking on the fog waves
i felt carried by the fog
I wanted to go to God
and the fogs knew it
So they carried me on

I walked and walked and walked
until I reached the pure white skies
They carried me in and brought me
to the golden gates of paradise

There I waited and waited
for those emotional moments
when God will come down
to receive me and to lead me
to His sacred throne of love.

AT THE FOOT OF MOUNT SINAI

Lost in silent meditation
I sat at the foot of Mount
From the top of Sinai
I heard this call
As the dawn burst into
Golden streams of light

An unknown Voice told me
"I am the God of Moses
Love and love until you die".

At your death bed
I shall come to you
and I shall lift you
up into my world of Angels
and keep you near my heart
for all eternity

I am love
Pure love
Come my son
Love.

STORM IN THE SEA

They were travelling in a boat
Crossing the Sea of Galilee
Suddenly there arose a storm
from the dark underbelly of the sea
slapping the boat on its sides
and a furious squall came up
waves breaking all over and across
and the boat was about to capsize

Imagine yourself in that boat
a sturdy vessel made of wood
but no match for those giant waves
towering ten feet on all your sides

Suddenly the mighty force in full wrath
descends cascading from the top
and the boat topples and its bent bow
points straight into darkening sky

And when you fear getting flipped
over backward into the devouring sea
the vessel pitches forth with a jolt
into belly of another wave on the rise

And they cried out in fear:
"Teacher, don't you care
if we all drown in the sea?"

The teacher said nothing
He just waved his hand
And the sea was calm.

(Poet's Note :- Master commanded and the sea became calm - Mark 4: 38)

NO MANTRA NO MAGIC WAND

He didn't chant a mantra
nor wave a wand
No angels were called
no help was needed
The raging water became
a stilled sea, instantly.

Immediate calm
Not a ripple. Not a drop
Not a gust
In a moment the sea
went from a churning
torrent to a peaceful pond

He got up, rebuked
the wind and said
to the waves, 'Quiet!
Be still!'

Then the wind died down
and it was completely calm.

He said to His disciples,
'Why are you so afraid?
Do you still have no faith?

(Mark 4: 39-40)

ON THE BANKS OF GANGES

On the banks of river Ganges
I sat in a serene sombre mood
Looking at the playful ripples
As the wind like a great artist
Drew playful lines and circles
On the surface of the water

The titillating wind
Tickles the water
And it laughs merrily
Although I cannot hear
When the water laughs
And jumps, it moves
In wavy lines and circles
And then it rushes
Swiftly to the shore

I sit there at the shore
With my feet in water
Watching the lines and circles
I reach and kiss my feet
In reverent love

The wind is playful today
And it comes to my lips
With a cold feathery touch
And it caresses my hair
And I feel alive again
It tells me about the sweet words
Uttered by lovers on the shore
Sharing their intimate feelings

Tonight I shall dream again

Of the symphony of the dancers
And I shall weave my fairy tale
In which lovers will come to this shore
Kissing a thousand kisses
Telling their stories of love
Smiling and lazing
On the lap of each other

I wish you O Divine Lovers
On this love sprinkled shore
Bliss, serenity and peace
Come sleep here lovingly
Sleep the night through
Let the glorious moon
Pour its mild honey
And heavenly light on you

Sleep together lovingly
In the arms of God.

IN TWINKLING DELIGHT

The soft moonbeams
fell in love with the earth

And the earth responded
Beaming with smiles
Wreathed in soft light

Still I see in my dreams
how the moonlight hugs
the earth in intimate love

The angel of love pours down
stardust in inexpressible love

In twinkling delight
my heart jumps for joy.

DEW DROPS AND STARLIGHT

Dewdrops and starlight
danced in my being
deep down in tandem
in the valley of my soul

They sang the love songs
of an eternal romance
of the soul and the creator
locked in sweet embrace

And the angels sing
in moonlight tonight
my soul still dreams
of the dance of divine
and the dew drops
and starlight smile.

O RAIN CLOUDS

Rain clouds
would you sing to me
a song of love?

I need a song
I need a flower
I need a shining star
to bring me
to the gratification
of my deep cravings

Rain clouds
would you sing to me
a song of love?

I need a song
I need a flower
I need a shining star
to bring me
to the satiation
of my deep cravings.

IN THE SILENT SHADE

Pensive do I sit
in the silent shade
of wishes unfulfilled

In moments of silence
I do count my wishes
The dead ones I send
For a silent burial
And the ones burning still
To my pensive heart

No matter how many wishes
You still have unfulfilled
If you have someone
Who loves you for what you are
Then your life is worth living.

DREAMS COME FROM HEAVEN

There is a land where dreams
dance in tremendous joy
They dance on angels' wings
on soft tails of white doves

They lie flat and sleep
on dancing feathers
of colored peacocks
and at birth of dusk
the dreams fly down
from heavenly caverns
to earth's sweet shore

As the moon shines
they begin to dance
on the shining waters
of mild flowing river
and in secret villages
where farmers sleep
and sheep cozily lie

Dreams do dance
on the lips of lovers
who spend their nights
on the river banks
hugging and kissing
giggling and hissing

Dreams come from heaven
to make love a dream
God cares for you and me
he puts you and me
in motions of heavenly love.

(Poet's Note :- I published it In Starlite Cafe under name of my mother Genova)
Editor's Note :- The poet never had any physical mother named Genova

IN MY SANDALWOOD GARDEN

I built a small straw hut
In my sandalwood garden
Where the wind fell in love
With my sandalwood trees

Wind comes to visit sandal
Still every now and then here
In morning, noon and at dusk
Wind comes stealthily at night
To visit his lady love, The Sandal

Why would I need a mansion?
I sleep in my small straw hut
In peace, breathing always
The sandal perfume
Which the wind steals
From his lady love.

HOW GOD SAVED ISRAEL

God Who saved His people of Israel
from despair in Egypt
after four hundred years of bondage

The shed blood of Passover lambs
applied on their doors
gave true picture of Passover Lamb

Whose holy blood shed at Calvary
healed the entire nation
by saving people from slavery to sin

He would come as Horn of Salvation
for the lost sheep of Israel

He would come to heal the nation
from its spiritual sickness

He would come to wake His people
From spiritual slumber

And remove their blinkers
from spiritual blindness.

FROM THE MOUNT OF SINAI

Clouds, thunder, lightning, rain
This holy season of penitence
God comes from Mount of Sinai
Awe-inspiring is his presence

Sing us a glorious tune
Play on your wild harps
Dance in His presence
With a heart full of joy

Glory of the Lord
Pillar of the cloud
For the Most High
From Mount Sinai
God comes down
To human beings
He will not deny

He appeared to Moses, Aaron, Joshua
He answered Job out of tempest
He came to Moses in the burning bush
He wrestled with Jacob till daybreak

Come let us adore our Lord
Hindu, Moslem, Buddhist, Christian
Come let us all adore the One
Almighty God who is the savior
The sole truth beyond all religion.

BEAUTIFUL DREAMER

Walk down to me
Beautiful dreamer
Collect the dewdrops
On a smoothie leaf
Come give it to me

O sing to me
Beautiful dreamer
Sing in moonlight
Songs of romance
In soft melody.

ALONG THE RIVER BANKS

Along the river banks
I strolled for a while
lost in meditative thoughts
behind my outer smile

I looked at the beauty
of the distant mountains
gasping at the greatness
of God playing with nature

The beauties of creation
brooks bubbling with life
clouds pregnant with rain
the seasons, the colours
the love birds in motion
proclaimed glory of God

I wonder at the heart of God
from where all these beauties
flow down like a magic to us.

ON TOP OF MISTY MOUNTAINS

On the top of misty mountains
I sat in peace and inner joy
I pierced through the skies
And saw the heavens opening

Heavenly beings were coming down
in glorious attires of so many hues
Along the slopes of misty mountains
I waited and waited in the morning
till the day sky took on myriad colors
and sprinkled on my heart and body
the sense of the joy of the colors.

I had a longing never to climb down
from the top of my misty mountain
but to sit there silently day and night
to watch every dawn and dusk play

I am sure one fine mystic moment
God will come down from heavens
on the top of my misty mountains
to show his benevolent face
to this deeply yearning heart
Oh God, don't you know that
I have such a longing for you?

HEART OF THE SEA

The heart of the sea
hums secret love songs
I had never heard of
In my mountain abode

I want to fill the nooks
of my mountain of silence
with the secret humming
of the soulful sea

And every dusk I fly
down to the shores
To collect the sweet
hummings of the sea

And the whole night I fly
back to my mountains
regaled with hums of sea

This flight with the hums
of the seas in my heart
gives me joy immeasurable.

HE ROWED ME INTO OBLIVION

I stood all alone
on my forlorn shore
as the moon shone

My eyes were closed
In a mystified mood

My heart was filled
with joy of silence
And I heard the music
of silence
deep down in my soul

God came to my shore
In his boat rowing silently
I heard the silent sounds
of ripples as God came

I opened my closed eyelids
God nodded inviting me to his boat
As if pushed by someone behind me
I went and stepped into his boat

He rowed silently
Through miles of silence
It was a soul consoling silence

We went far away from my shore
I turned back and saw that shore
far, far away moving away from me
in constant rhythms of the ripples
created by Him while rowing

All the way down to the center
of the sea where waves did not move
I felt the soft mild wind talking to me
heavenly things which I did not understand

He rowed and rowed,
did not talk a word.
I heard only his breath.

He looked at me
I looked at him
He smiled
I smiled

He rowed and rowed
me away from my shore.

I could not see the shore anymore
I was all alone with Him

Suddenly i felt his love
like the petals of devadaru

He smiled, I smiled
Tears fell from my eyes
I saw his tears too

He rowed and rowed
in silence that pierced my soul
into oblivion.

(Poet's Note :- This is a dream i had about my death.)

Editor's Note :- Devadaru or Cedrus deodara is a species of cedar native to the western Himalayas, known for its perfume and medicinal value. Hemangi Sharma's native place in Kashmir has it in abundance.)

REBUILD MY CHURCH

Francis, go rebuild my church,
which, as you see, is all in ruins.

Jesus spoke these words
Hundreds of years ago
To Saint Francis
of Assisi
from the crucifix
of the crumbling church
of San Damiano near Assisi.

How prophetic were the words
it was a pivotal moment
which changed the life of Francis
and changed the very course
of Christian history.

Love flowed from faith
Work flowed from love
Faith flowed from work
And church was rebuilt

A man of prayer will change the world
A man of power cannot.

PART – V

TEMPTATION OF GOD

SATAN AND HIS WORKING

Two is joy. In creation everything is created in only two. Even the sprouting bud comes in twos. Sun and moon, day and night, two ears, two nostrils, two eyes, two cheers, two legs, two hands, two lungs, two hearts make one love. Two breasts for a single child. Two ovaries for a single uterus, two cheeks for a single face. And Two was God split into when he wanted to make Love

For ages I have been kept hungry and imprisoned in a cave. Now you are filling the parched deserted heart with heavenly ambrosia. Oh god, when divine energies flood in, what could mortal souls say. Now you are feeding this famished soul, whose intestine's capacity is just a hole of blue sky and a pinch of golden sun light. You are filling my whole with ocean of love when my heart's capacity is that of a newborn baby to suckle just a drop of its flavour.

I am every day morning brushing their teeth, oiling their hair, combing, powdering, milking them, feeding them, clothing them, caressing and fondling them, laugh with them, show them sky, birds, mongoose, owls, bats and all that my eyes could see, sing songs to them, kiss them with my loving heart. What not I do for them. Now when I open my heart and show to you, you say oh, it is only a shoe flower..."

CAT AND FRIED FISH

The cat and the fried fish

My mother cooks well
She fried fish with different spices
Smell of it filled the whole house
Mummy kept the fried fish
On kitchen table and went.

The cat smelled and came
The cat came and saw
sprang on to the kitchen table.

Suddenly God commanded
Do not touch it !!!

Again the cat sprang
And God commanded
Do not touch it !!!

The cat could not resist
and reached the fried fish
It was so tempting
and God commanded
Do not eat the fried fish !!!

The cat paused
thought
listened
reflected
kept his tail down
head bowed
and stepped back

In a decisive moment
the cat turned back
and went away pensive

Being at peace now
the cat began to sing
Miaaaaawoooo

The angels heard it
heavenly choir began singing
in pleasant and varied notes:

Miahhaaa woooo Miaaaa woooo,
Miahhhaaaa woooo

The cat and God smiled.

(Poet's Note :- When we have sexual temptations, God tells us 'Do not touch'.
Would you become then the CAT in my poem?)

'I say unto you, that likewise joy shall be in heaven over one sinner that repenteth,
more than over ninety and nine just persons, which need no repentance'. (The
Holy Bible - Luke : 15.7)

THE ARCHER'S SHOT

Of success in life
Great Chinese Sage
Tranxu said this:

When archer shoots
for no particular prize
he has all his skills

But when he shoots to win
a golden trophy, the first prize
he goes blind, prize disturbs him
He sees two targets
One which is present
One which is absent
Drained of his concentration
He becomes out of mind

His skill is the same
But prize divides him

He thinks more of winning
than shooting with all skill

A divided mind is
the Satan's mind

Take up a single arrow
And with a single shot
Pierce the eye of your Fish.

(Editor's Note :- Arjuna in the epic Mahabharata could pierce the eye of the fish
with a single arrow to obtain Draupadi, the Panchala princess as wife. Unlike the
other suitor kings, Arjuna was not after Draupadi or the Panchala kingdom. He was
unattached, and hence victorious.)

YOU DUPED ME LORD

'You duped me, Lord'
Jeremiah shouted out in the desert

Jeremiah the most tender and loving
cried out against God

'You have cheated me God
Everyone mocks me now
I am an object of laughter
You are too strong for me
And you always triumph

I want to go away from God
I don't want to be a prophet
I will not speak in God's name
Never, never, never, anymore'.

But Oh Lord, O Lord, dear Lord !!

Love of God is like a burning fire
Burning in my heart's chamber
and imprisoned in my bones

O God, you are my God
whom my soul seeks
for you my flesh pines
and my soul thirsts.

How shall I forsake my God?

(Poet's Note :- Dedication implies sacrifice. Married people may think of their mutual commitment in love. Children and parents, if committed to mutual happiness in the family, may think of their daily living under one roof. Love means giving of self. Self-giving is a source of happiness.)

Editor's Note :- Jeremiah the Prophet of the Old Testament prophesied as he was inspired by God. But he was imprisoned and suffered a lot. When Priest Pashhur, son of Immer, heard Jeremiah prophesying, he had him beaten and put in the stocks at Upper Gate of Benjamin at the Lord's temple. At first Jeremiah cried loud against God but later came to God again in love. (Reference: Jeremiah 20: 1-9)

HEAD OF MEDUSA

The glorious saga of hero Perseus
Is still recounted by ancient Greeks
As he sat at the wedding supper
With lovely Andromeda by his side

The hall's door was torn open
Another king appeared with arms
To take away Andromeda by force
A wild fight ensued
Many fell by the sword
Enemies were large in numbers
It was Perseus' moment of truth

And he called to his enemies:
"You force me to the utmost
and the most terrible! Perish!"
And as he holds a bag
that hangs on his side
he exclaims: "Turn away his face!"

And his hand holds up aloft
the horrible head of Medusa
the terrible monster with a corpse's smell
instead of hair she had snakes on her head

Whoever saw her face froze to stone
A look at Medusa killed them forever.

(Poet's Note :- The Gospel tells about a head of the dead whose sight gives
eternal life until this day. At that time Jesus spoke to Nicodemus: As Moses
raised the serpent in the wilderness, so Son of Man must be raised, so that
everyone who believes in him has eternal life in him" - John, 3:14-15).

(Editor's Note :- When Satan distracts the devotee from God, he has to strike a
death blow to Satan by showing his superior arsenal. Rising of the colled spiritual
power inside human spine is like the serpent raising its hood).

THEY WILL WALK LIKE BLIND

I will bring distress on men
so that they walk like blind
because they have sinned
against the Benevolent Lord

Their blood will be poured
out like dust into drains
and their flesh like dung

Such will be the time
when God will bring
such severe distress upon men
they will grope about begging
as if they are blind and lame

And that day of judgement
all these sinners shall see
because they have sinned
against the Benevolent Lord

Sin is terrible in the sight of God
because the price paid for that sin
is the precious blood of Jesus Lord
which was shed on Calvary's cross.

MY SENSE OF LOSS

(I lost my mother, my sister and my father)

I miss their laughter
and quick wit, still
living this life in exile
each of them loving me
in their own way

I miss the chance
they each gave me
to enter their worlds
to care for them

Their absence leaves
a dark hole in my heart
that will never be filled
in this world till I die

And I am grieving still
for their untimely loss
and time is taking time
to work through meanings
of what that great loss
still means to me.

(Editor's Note :- This poem was written in December 2019. At that time Antony Theodore aka Tony Brahmin aka Hemangi Sharma was not yet bereaved. Antony sings of everlasting love, and yet talks about pain of separation from human relatives. Obviously the poet is hinting about the illusion of human love.)

HOUND OF HEAVEN

All things will betray you
If you betray Me

I shall not relent
I shall give chase
Until you tire
Until you repent
And return to me

Nothing will ever shelter you
Who won't shelter Me

Now go away run
Go have your fun
Game will be on
At end of your game
You shall find me

I am the One you always seek
Even if you don't seek

I need not give chase
If you are on the chase
For lay life's trinkets
Each road you choose
Returns to me

All thirsting mouths shall seek me
When no worldly elixir will comfort
All pining hearts shall rest in me
When no earthly love will support.

(Poet's Note :- In The Hound of Heaven, Francis Thomson described with an almost terrible power, not the self's quest of adored Reality, but Reality's quest of the unwilling self. He shows to us the remorseless, tireless seeking and following of the soul by the Divine Life to which it will not surrender. This idea of the love chase, of the prodigal soul rushing in terror from the overpowering presence of God, but followed, sought, conquered in the end, is common to all the medieval mystics.)

SINNER WOMAN

A woman was caught in the act
And brought before Son of Man
Such adulterous woman in town
How shall the Word be protected
If she is not stoned now to death?

And He saw that darkness
lurking in the sinful hearts
of all those men and elders
Scribes and the Pharisees
who had accused her of sin

And a little later we read:
Jesus spoke to the Scribes
and said to the Pharisees
'I am the Light of the world
He who follows Me will not walk
ever in the path of darkness
but will have the Light of life'.

LIFE WITHOUT GOD

It's no life all, not at all
worse than even death
futile and meaningless
a life lived without God

All your efforts, desires
intellectual pursuits
seeking of pleasure
grabbing of powers
personal prestige
accumulation of wealth
all these are utterly vain

When Lord is eliminated
from the human heart
then the circle of life
and inevitability of death
express nothing in spirit
but hopelessness
said Solomon the Wise:

When God is excluded
you give your enemy
full sway on your life.

(Poet's Note :- Reference to Ecclesiastes 4: 9 in the Holy Bible).

HANDS OF SAVIOUR

He looked at her
For they all wanted
To stone her to death

But she was silent
For she had confessed
And the sin was gone

Jesus gave her his hand

His hand is the hand of deliverance
His hand is the hand of redemption

His hand saves you and me
from all our sins

He proclaimed:
'Throw the first stone at her
those amongst you
who have never sinned'.

She smiled, she cried
she jumped, she danced

She hugged the savior
And no stone was cast
When the savior loved.

SATAN'S TEMPT

When Satan confronted Jesus
He did not pick Him up
And throw from the pinnacle

Nor did he turn stone to bread
And stuff it in Jesus' mouth
He had no power to do that

He had to appeal to Jesus
And then wait his response

And what was the response?
It was not anything like
"Who do you think you are?
Do you know who I am
I am the Son of God

Jesus responded with Word of God:

Man shall not live by bread alone
But by very power of the Word
Man shall not put to test the Lord
And man shall serve the Lord alone

He spoke the scriptures directly
Using authority of God's Word
To defend Himself from Satan

All three temptations - same response:
"It is written. It is written. It is written."

Satan did not argue back
He simply left Jesus alone

at least for the time being

After the final temptation
in wilderness, we are told
"(devil) departed from Him
until an opportune time"

We are not told when and how
but the implication is so clear
Satan did come back to Him
Indeed, we can be sure of it
Satan was a constant companion
During the days of His flesh.

(Poet's Note :- He was never very far away – ref : Luke 4.13)

Editor's Note :- The Satan of Bible and Qu'ran is the same as Maya of Hindu
scriptures – the divisive force which creates the illusion of separate existence

MIND OF SATAN

It is hard to read Satan's mind
He didst think of tricking Jesus
To get a few more dark millennia
Of the rule of evil over the world
Before he met his final destiny

But whatever was his design
Satan was disappointed sorely
For Jesus foretold His disciples
Before His arrest in Gethsemane
That ruler of this world was coming
And that he had nothing in Him

Was Satan searching for a hole
A crack, a chink, a loophole
Any something in Jesus's mind
He wanted to enter Jesus' mind
Just as he entered Eve's mind

And this is surely the real story
Of the Garden of Gethsemane
It was the last and final struggle
Between Jesus and the Satan.

ALTAR WAS CLOSED TO KING

King Uzzia once the obedient
became powerful and haughty
he went to Temple of Yahweh
all by himself to burn incense
on the altar that was holy.

It's not for you O King Uzziah
To burn incense on this altar
Priests from Aron's descent
Are alone consecrated for this
Eighty priests warned the king
Led by Azariah the high priest
The king had no right to enter
and burn incense on holy altar

But mighty Uzzia won't listen
Who can be greater than me
I am the king of this land
He argued with the priests
And incense burner in hand
He stepped into the altar

And at that moment earth shook
Sun blazed full on Uzzia's face
Leprosy broke out on his forehead
And he had to leave that altar
Never to step in a temple again
Uzzia was human and unclean
Soon enough he lost the throne.

(Poet's Note :- Uzziah was struck with leprosy for disobeying God – Holy Bible :- 2 Kings 15.5; 2 Chronicles 26.19-21. Thiele dates the incident to 751/750 BC).

Editor's Note :- This legend signified that devotion and spirituality ultimately triumph over material possessions and brute power.

PROSTITUTES YOU LOVED

Lepers were your friends
You touched their wounds
You healed them and hugged them
Their skin creamed without blemish

And to the prostitutes you said
"My dears, don't sin again"
Blessing them with your right arm
They smiled in your presence
They knew beauty of true love

Your simplicity of life
Is the light to our paths
In this mad material world
You did feed the poor
You cared for the needy
Adorned with the feathers
Of kindness and love.

You are my Christ whom i adore
You are my Christ whom i adore.

MY TEARS AND MY DREAMS

I collected all my tears
In a dry coconut shell
And they glittered in sunshine
You know my tears
Have dazzle of diamonds

I gathered all my dreams
In a little thin plastic bag
And kept it under my armpit
You know my dreams
Have the colour of gold

I ran as fast as I could
to the King's Palace.
for I wanted to sell
my tears and dreams
my mother was dying
I had no money
for her medicine

The Guards waved their swords
And I begged 'allow me please'.

On the courtyard I stood
i the beggar of mercy
And the princess in whites
Came down and asked
Why are you here?
My mother is dying I said
I would like to sell .....

What?

My tears, I said
You know they are diamonds.
I have my dreams too
You know they are all gold

My mother is dying... i cried.

Princess burst into tears
She hugged me, like this
It was so intense
She caressed my hair
Her hands ran down my face
And touched my lips wet
With the salt of my tears

The King saw, came down
Swirled his mighty sword
And with a single blow
My head rolled down
Did the princess' head roll down too?

I still remember how sweet her hugs were
How lovingly she did touch me
How she looked into my eyes
With such tender passion
Do you know how I still remember?

YOU SAW ME BUT DID NOT CURE

I was a beggar whose foot was cut off
I was the woman whom people called a prostitute
I was the child on the homeless street
I was the one who fell at your feet
for a bowl full to eat

You saw me and did not care

I was in ragged clothes
I had no shoes and walked in rain
I was poor and cried on the road
I was the school girl who had no books

You saw me and did not car.

I came to you several times
today knocking at your door
You were too busy to notice

I went away sad from your door.

CLOUDS OF DESPAIR

The clouds of despair
are gathering momentum

Who says
Come not nigh
Come not nigh

Clouds will not darken
my light filled mind

I enchant deep within me
whispers of blooming
petals of purity

I pray on my knees
for rainbows of hope
to shine on this sanctuary
of my soul offering blossoms
in murmuring prayerful silence.

TRUTH IN A SKULL

Like skulls and bones
All your earthly wealth
Great beauty and health
Will remain strewn
And rot on this earth
When you depart

Where is Isabella now
And her legendary beauty
Where are her suitors
Who lined up with flowers
Under her balcony

All dead, all gone
What is left on earth
Of their royal romance
Are skulls and bone

Cling on to Christ
Your eternal friend
And the Supreme Lover
God's extended hand
As your love's lone guide

"Only one petty life
It will soon be past
Only what is done
For Christ will last."

(Poets' Note :- A sixteenth-century Jesuit saint, Francis Borgia, held a skull in his hand and spent a life in meditation and charity. During his youth, when he was a rich businessmen, he once saw the decomposing remains of the Empress Isabella, and was shaken to his core and bones. Then he decided to serve God alone, rather than temporary things.)

FALSE GODS

In fear I hid myself
inside a cave in darkness

In diffidence I dared not
look into the light

I was a broken person
bereft of vocation

Then He came to me
shining in His own Light

He found me as He had found
Gideon in the cave

He found me as He had found
lost sheep among the thorns

And I was carried on His shoulder
on the greater path of Victory.

Editor's Note :- There was a man named Gideon among Israelites who did not want to worship any but Yahweh. One day he was threshing wheat by the wine-press to hide it from the Midianites. An angel of the Lord appeared and spoke to him, saying, "The Lord is with you, mighty man of valor, and you have been chosen to save Israel." The next day Gideon took ten of his servants and went up to the hill on which an altar had been erected to the false gods whom the people were worshiping. He threw down the false altars and built an altar to God in the same place, and on it he made a burnt offering to God. (Book of Judges : Ch-6)

PART – VI

THE FINAL CROSS

TWILIGHT OF LIFE AND DEATH

You are the god I was searching for. What more could I say. If a human heart could be divine, if god is born as human and if you could sense his heart, then it is yours. I had never in the horizon of my dreams horizon ever dreamed that a man could be as divine as you. And to be truthful, the man behind the curtain of god, I kneel before him too.

Never, never shall I betray you. Though a lamb you are a lamp. You are my dearest Jesus. You are the lone light at the top of my temple. And I shall never never even show you any cross at all. You see, I am the biggest cross in the world. Then you know, this cross if you wear, if you endure, then no cross will be more difficult for you to bear.

The cross will be thrown out soon. And it will have to walk to the cross bearer in the middle of night. Hope the cross bearer will come riding a white peacock to me....

You are my be-all and end-all.

WHY AM I ALIVE

Lord, God
why am I alive?
Why didn't I die
at the moment
of my birth?

Why did you create
me to suffer?

I am drinking
and eating my tears
every day and night
Where are you my God?

After a while he answered:
"I am on the cross".

HOW THEY CRUCIFY THE LORD

The cross is placed on the ground.

The exhausted man is quickly thrown backward with his shoulders again the wood. The legionnaire feels for the depression at the front of the wrist. He drives a heavy, square wrought-iron nail through the wrist and deep into the wood. Quickly he moves to the other side and repeats the action, being careful not to pull the arms too tightly, but to allow some flex and movement.

The cross is then lifted into place.

The left foot is pressed backward against the right foot, and with both feet extended, toes down, a nail is driven through the arch of each, leaving the knees flexed.

The victim is now crucified.

As he slowly sags down with more weight on the nails in the wrists, excruciating, fiery pain shoots along the fingers and up the arms to explode in the brain. The nails in the wrists are putting pressure on the median nerves.

He pushes himself upward. Upward.

To avoid the stretching torment, he places the full weight on the nail through his feet. Again he feels the searing agony of the nail tearing through the nerves between the bones of his feet.

Pain ripples through the body.

As the arms fatigue, cramps sweep through the muscles, knotting them in deep, relentless, throbbing pain. With these cramps comes the inability to push himself upward to breathe. Air can be drawn into the lungs but not exhaled. He fights to raise himself in order to get even one small breath. Finally, carbon dioxide builds up in the lungs and in the bloodstream. Spasmodically he is able to push himself upward to exhale and bring in life-giving oxygen.

Hours of this pain. Hours of agony.

Cycles of twisting, joint-rending cramps, intermittent partial asphyxiation, and then searing pain as tissue is torn from his lacerated back as he moves up and down against the rough timber.

Then another agony begins:

A deep, crushing pain deep in the chest as the pericardium slowly fills with serum and begins to compress the heart.

It is now almost over.

The loss of tissue fluids has reached critical level.
The compressed heart is struggling to pump heavy, thick, sluggish blood into the tissues. The tortured lungs are making a frantic effort to gasp in small gulps of air.
He can feel the chill of death creeping through his tissues.

And He knows it
Just as it was written
Finally he can allow his body to die

So that he can rise.

(Poet's Note :- And they crucified Him -The Holy Gospel according to Mark 15: 24)

I DANCE ON ONE LEG NOW

I lift up my eyes to you
then lifting up my hands
and even legs one by one
standing on tip of my toe
like the Indian sanyasins

Like a yogi and a sadhu
in your unseen presence
I shall now begin my dance
before forgetting myself

Would you come to me
dancing in prema bhav
in affection, in emotion
in virtue and kindness
compassion, in eros
in creative intimacy.

(Editor's Note :- Just like standing on one leg is a penance for Hindu monks, suffering on the cross is also a penance for the devout Christians. The use of Sanskrit words reveal Antony's real identity as Hemangi Sharma.)

Prema = love
Bhav = feeling
Sadhu = ascetic; mendicant

VISION AT NIGHT

I gazed into the visions of the night
I saw a golden throne
All around was fire
It was a blaze of flames

A stream of fire and flames
poured out from His Presence

He was beyond all religions
beyond all the concepts of God

He was free from the thoughts of man
He was above everything

I gazed into the visions of the night
Millions waited on him

On the clouds of heaven I saw
a shining white robed being
he came and opened my book of life.

He looked with fire in His eyes
and hugged me in intense love

It was a mystery, it was pure joy
I fell in His benevolent presence.

THRONE OF LIGHT

When the spring rains came
I stood at the doorsteps
of my little hut in the woods

I saw my moist heart
glistening in the mild rain drops

I am waiting here to be suckled
oh invisible little fairy

Leave imprints on me, in me

Fill my eager mouth
with the pot of potion
of living romance

Suckle the nectar
of my lonely heart-flower

Leave it wet by your soaking lips

See my sorrowful heart
and lead me
to the throne of light.

KING LED ME TO LIGHT

Clothed in fire and flame
sharing His splendour
He came, the Adorable

With majesty enrobed
the king of the universe
robed himself with might

Anguished and alone
i stood transfixed
singing His praises
with a burning soul

The King's eternal gates
opened for me

I saw his throne
flooded in endless light

The King led me into light.

FLESH OF MY FLESH

Flesh of my flesh,
soul of my soul,
blood of my blood,
wounds of my wounds,
i am ready to die for you
on the holy cross.

By your Word alone i live
By your Love alone i sing

Beat of my heart
Pulse of my life
Shine of my eyes
Pull of my breath
I am ready to live for you
To carry your cross.

IF YOU TAKE AWAY MY BREATH

If you take away my breath
I will fall down and perish
My body shall return to dust

I feel your life-giving breath
when in early spring
nature wakes me up
from winter's sleep

Your love alone can renew
the face of this earth

I shall open my mouth
and gladly praise you my Lord

Your love endures forever.

JOURNEY OF MY SOUL

The journey of my soul has begun
And my cup overflows

My lyre plays in the silence of night
My flute has melodies unheard

My spirit grows closer to God

The lamp of glory burns in me
in the deepest caverns of my soul

Watch !!
I am going with feathery steps
to the world of holy saints

Look !!
Journey of my soul has begun
In the sanctuary of my devotions

(Poet's Note :- I want to welcome death. I am not at all afraid to die. My greatest consolation is my faith in an after-life in the world of God, where my cup will continue to overflow.)

MY CHALICE OF GLORY

When I wanted to lift up
the Chalice of Glory
my God told me:
"You should suffer".

I asked him why?

He told me:
Only through sufferings
one can achieve glory

Suffering produces endurance
Endurance produces character
Character produces hope
Hope does not put us to shame
because God's love has been
poured into our hearts
through Spirit of the Almighty.

God will himself restore,
confirm, strengthen,
and establish you

And then you can lift up
the Chalice of Glory.

YOU WILL BE WITH ME

There were three on the crosses
of the Calvary hill

The evil thief mocked
'Come down from the cross
you Almighty Jesus
save yourself and us'.

The good thief said
'Lord remember me
when you are in paradise'.

Lord Jesus from the cross
uttered in deep love:
'Truly i say to you
you will be with me
today in paradise'.

Love conquers evil
Goodness conquers all
Strength and faith in God
shall conquer you.

COME HEAL ME

I want healing
Come and touch me
with your healing hand
Heal me now.

You ask me 'do you believe?
Do you have enough faith? '
I still have doubt
I have many doubts

Seeing my thoughts, God tells:

'I cannot heal you now,
you have to believe in me,
in my healing power,
in my great desire to be with you'.

'Believe in my love for you
Love yourself as you are
and come to me in faith'.

'Kneel down in prayer full of faith
I shall heal you'.

CAN I KNOW

Can the 'I' know itself?
Can the knife cut itself?
Can the tooth bite itself?
Can the eye see itself?
Can the "I" know itself?

As I come closer
And closer to you
Lord I do not see
Who I am

DREAMS CRY

Dreams cry in me
The angels hear it
Desires are burning in me
like fire in the air

Tears dry on me
The angels see it
Hopes are radiating still
Like light from candle

Who will quench my thirst?
Would you my dearest angel?

RESCUE ME LORD

God,
I have lost my way in a barren desert
Rescue me in my peril

I live in darkness and gloom
I feel I am bound in chains

I was proud
You humbled my heart through hardships

In my distress I cry to you
Break my chains asunder

Speak to me your loving word
to heal my heart and soul
I shall praise the wonders of God
in the barren desert

Calm the storm wind in me
Hush the storm to a murmur

You who can change rivers into desert,
change my desert into pools of water.

WOUNDED AND TORMENTED

Christ became like us,
took birth and died
got exposed to grueling powers
in fight with those who love the lie,
got surrounded by people
who barely understood him,
got wounded, tormented
and crucified.

He lived in conflict,
he was tried
and abandoned

He went to the basics
of all things he saw
with the question: Why?

His answer encourages us to live

He gave us his word
that dispels all fear
that frees us from doubt
and enables hope.

AKIBA ON DEATH BED

Akiba was on his deathbed,
He bemoaned to his rabbi
"Rabbi, i am a failure
I have not done anything
Achieved anything in my life.
Why should I live like this?"

Rabbi moved closer to him
and asked why.

Akiba confessed:
"I did not live a life like Moses
I am just a failure in life".
The poor man began to cry
He said: "I fear God's judgement".

The rabbi hugged him
and told in his ear softly:
"God will not judge Akiba
for not being Moses
God will judge Akiba
for not being Akiba".

LORD ACCEPT MY LOVE

Lord, please accept
my little offering of love

i give you a lotus,
blooming flower of grace and glory
to you and offer it at your holy feet

Lift me up from my darkness
and the dirt from which i try to rise
to become a beautiful lotus
to dance in your presence.

THE PILLAR OF LIGHT

Immaculee Ilibagiza remembers
She was gasping for breath in her small hole
Packed like sardines with her six friends
Her killers were just a gunshot away
Yet she felt God was so close to her
When night was dark she saw that light

I felt the fear pumping through my veins
My blood was on fire, I struggled to meditate
I struggled to form an image of God in my mind

And then that image got formed
Two pillars of brilliant white light
Burning before me like two giant legs
I wrapped my arms around those legs
Like a frightened child clinging to her mother
I begged God to fill me with his light
To cast out darkness from my heart

I am holding to you my dear God
I do not doubt you can save me
I am not going to let go of you
Until you send the killers away

She became a source of light
And hope of her companions
And the killers all went away.

(Poet's Note :- During the Rwandan genocide in 1994, Immaculee Ilibagiza and seven other women were forced to hide and huddle silently together in a cramped bathroom three feet by four feet for 91 days. She said she was saved by her constant meditation on Christ, which took the shape of two pillars of light constantly burning before her like two giant legs.)

Editor's Note :- When Immaculee finally came out of her hole, she found her entire family massacred. But she forgave their killers.

I SEE YOU BEHIND CLOSED EYES

Closing my eyes
i see you standing before me
Closing my ears
i hear your melodious voice

Closing my heart
i feel you inside my heart
dancing to the rhythms
of an unknown melody
which heavenly beings
alone can sing.

HOW MY GOD LOOKED

I sat on the banks of this river
I wanted to throw a little stone
to see the never ending ripples

But did not throw
for I feared
I might kill the joy
of the tranquil waters

In a moment I fell into a trance
I saw the river flooded with light
God appeared on the tranquil waters

I saw my God, I saw my God
He smiled at me
An unforgettable smile

Can you tell me dear
how my God looked like?

SEA OF LIGHT

Look, there is a sea of light
falling on the verdant hills
how it enters the silent valley

In her eager search after beauty
light reaches the wild flowers

I breathe the smell of glory

Wind plays on the silvery leaves
of the mighty redwoods in the valley
like an appetent lover full of mirth

The early morning haze lies
like a lovely spun yarn waiting
for the playful hands of her lover

The hazes of the dawn
like feathers of sun rays
fly softly in the clear air

The silver grey horizon
mirrors His endlessness

My soul drinks of the joy
flowing from that eternity.

O HUNTER

I am a little bird
I have lovely feathers
I attract many lovers
I am so beautiful

But there are many
who come after me
to hunt me down

God, my Lord
will save me from
the hunter's sling

I will not be ruined
while God protects me

His wings are my shield
I shall ever be faithful
observing the law of God

I shall please my God always
This is my life, ever protected
and I shall be always happy
in the safety of my Protector.

GOD SAW MY LONELY BOAT

My God saw me
and my lonely boat
from afar

He flew down to me
on angel wings
to love me
to caress me
and care for me

In my lonely moments
I see him flying to me
on wings of fire

That is my consolation

I shall never be left alone
never, never, never
and I shall always smile
a lovely smile that touches
the core of your heart.

HIGHER THAN HIGH, LOWER THAN LOW

I have gone up to the highest
that I have, and beheld
the Word of God
towering yet higher still

My curiosity took me
to my lowest depths
to look for Him
but he was nowhere
He was reaching down
deeper still

If I looked outside me
I found Him not
He was beyond my farthest
if I looked within
He was.

HE CAME IN THE NIGHT

He came at night
in the middle of night
all alone to me
in the midst of all that
dark troubled waters

He came to meet me
to talk to me
to hug me
to caress me
and console me

He came in the dark
in the middle of the dark
moments of my troubles
and He always still comes
in the darkest moments.

WE THREE

There were three on the crosses
of the Calvary hill.

The evil thief mocked Jesus
'Come down from the cross
you Almighty Jesus
save yourself and us'.

The good thief said.
'Lord remember me
when you are in paradise'.

Lord from the cross
uttered in deep love:
'Truly i say to you
you shall be with me
today in paradise'.

Love conquers evil
Goodness will conquer
All human hearts
And strength and faith
in God shall protect you.

MOUTHS OF CHRIST

Mama told me,
Remember, my son
all mouths are your
brothers and sisters.

You can't put something
in your own little mouth
without giving something
to someone somewhere
who is hungry and thirsty

Even through hardship of poverty
mother formed in us habits
and actions of solidarity
which was all charity
in Jesus Christ.

HIS WIDOWED MOTHER

Woman, here is your son
Said the dying son of man
As he hung from the cross
And looking as his disciple
John he commanded then
Look, here is your mother

O hypocritical Pharisees
you speak of rules and rules
but how did you treat
your widows your women
how indifferent you were
to the needs of women

Even as He hung
from the wooden cross
Christ's compassion flowed
Towards the widowed mother

And he made sure
John was there
to take her care
when he was no more
in her advancing years.

Editor's Note :- Holy Bible states that when Jesus was on the cross, he assigned
to John the duty of taking care of his widowed mother Mary (John 19.26-27)

CAST IN A PRISON

Behold !!!
Devil is about to cast you
and some of your men
into prison cells
you will be tested
you will have tribulation
for ten days of darkness

Be faithful !!!
Follow the Word
until death
and I shall give you
the crown of life

Living faithfully
for the Lord dearest
will not exempt us
from persecution
for Lord too suffered

All those who live
here godly lives
will suffer persecution

Do not fear
what you are
about to suffer

Fear not
and stand
firm in your faith.

BREATH OF LIFE

I open your graves
In the dead of night
and bring you up
like dried collar bones
out of your graves

I breathe my spirit
into your parched heart
and it comes to life
and then I bring you
back to life

Then you will see
that I am the Lord
and I am the Word
that you had heard

I have now spoken
you have heard
and I am doing it.

I AM FLOATING

Shapes and colors
vivid like dreams
appear in me
like torrents of joy

I feel I am floating
on a bed of light
like a feather of love
in rapturous delight

I thank the world
I thank all souls
rivers and trees
birds and beasts

I and you are one
our souls are one
our heart and mind
breath and pulse
joy and sorrow
are one

with this feeling
of oneness in me
I float serenely
like a dream.

PRAYER FROM CATACOMB

In the Catacombs of Callixtus
a woman prayed in an antique age
her picture is on the walls
her head covered with a veil
wearing a costly vestment
but opening up her palms
like a shell of two halves
she lifts up her hands to God
lifting us all up to heaven
as if she prays for all of us

Women and men of all religions
have lifted up their hands
opening up their palms
to Gods and Goddesses
since the antique age

Here in the Catacomb
still lives that antique woman
in the underground dark cemetery
praying at the face of death and graves

O Hindus, Muslims, Christians
Jews, Buddhists and Jains
men of all religions come
we shall lift up our hands
and spread them like open shells
God who is beyond all religions
will listen to our prayers
for unity and harmony.

(Poet's Note :- There is a mural painting of a praying woman from third century
visible even now in the underground cemetery of the catacomb in Rome. This
poem was written after seeing it)

ST AUGUSTINE WRITES

I entered into secret
closet of my soul
led by Thee, I entered
because you were my helper
I entered and beheld
with mysterious eye of my soul
the Light that never changes
the light above the eye
of my soul
above my intelligence

and it was not the common light
which all flesh can see
nor was it greater yet of the same kind
as if the light of day were to grow brighter
and brighter and flood all space
It was not like this
but different altogether
different from all such things
Nor was it above my intelligence
in same way as oil is above water
or heaven above the earth
but it was higher because it made me
and I was lower because made by it

He who knows the Truth
knows that One Light
and who knows it
knows eternity

Love knows it.

(Poet's Note :- St. Augustine, Confessions, Bk. vii Chp. XI)

PRAISE TO LORD

Praise Jehovah from the heavens
Praise ye Him in the heights
Praise Him all His angels
Praise Him all His host
Praise Him sun and moon
Praise Him all ye stars of light

Praise Him you heavens of heavens
and all you waters that are
above the heavens.

Let them praise
the Name of Jehovah
for HE commanded
and they were created
He set them there forever
and ever and gave a law

and not one transgresseth it.

[Poet's Note :- Reference to Psalm 148 of the Holy Bible]

PART – VII

THE AFTER LIFE

PROMISES OF ETERNITY

HOUSE OF MY BELOVED

Whatever you give, you receive in thousand folds. If you give with a pure heart and a pure mind with pure intentions, when you are sharing your love, your whole being will be flooded with that Love.

Now I know, when I met you, that there is this god whom I had prayed all these days. See, with meeting you the whole thing is over. Now living is the plum of cake. You are asking will I eat the cake or not. See, if I eat it will be finished. So I will only lick and keep on licking so that the cake is okay. I can have the cake and lick the cake.

I want to go to my Beloved's house and die there itself, never to come back again. But when you go to the moon, you will realise that moon is like earth only…..

Love is not mine, neither yours, you cannot possess it, nor can you dispossess it. Every pure mind is permeable to love that flows through it. Like water that runs across when there are no dams, like rivers that flow through forests and wilds, love just flows through hearts when there is no barrier.

DYING I ENTER MY HOME

On the white sands of the shore
There a came a wave
It came up to my feet
touched my feet
and washed it

Receding,
it gave me
bubbles and white foam
dying instantly
as it joined the mighty sea

The sea is my home
By dying on the shore
I enter my home.

SOUL AND FLAMING IRON

A black piece of iron
becomes bright
to become a piece of fire

Behold it
the penetrating fire
shines through the iron
that it gives light

The iron does not cease
to be iron
and source of the fire
also retains
its own identity

Fire does not take iron into it
but penetrates and shines through it
It is iron as it was before
so also is the source of fire

And such is the relation
of our soul with God
God penetrates through soul
and dwells in the soul
but soul retains its identity

Soul may not comprehend God
but God comprehends the soul
God does not alter it
from being a soul
but only gives it
its divine source
and glory of the Majesty.

PRISONER'S FLUTE

I went to visit
a friend in prison

He smiled a lovely smile
greeting me in joy
and thanking me

He was so lonely
for days and nights
are very long in a prison

And so he smiled
and his eyes shone
with gratitude

Then he took his flute
his only companion
and began to play
songs of love

As he played I thought
he was praying to God

He told he believed
angels listened to him
when he played
on his solitary flute

And at night
lovely fairies
with wings of gold
came to him
to sleep with him.

ANGEL OF LIGHT AND BEAUTY

I see the angel
walking to me

Angel of light
Angel of beauty

I see the angel
smiling at me

Angel of joy
Angel of peace

Look ! Can you see?
Or only i am seeing?

The angel is coming to me
Angel of beauty and light

Do you think O Poetess
that the angel will now
speak to me?

What will the angel say?
How shall i answer?

NECTAR MOON

Look !!!
The full moon, tonight
pours down nectar

My soul knows no satiety
as i drink my nectar

The pores of my heart
fill with nectar moon

Drunk with moon tonight
my heart dances in joy

In my nectar filled heart
I begin to perceive
the moonlit smile
of God.

TWILIGHT KISS

In the twilight of tenderness
would you come and kiss me
on my lips of passionate desire

I wait for those moments
in which your horizon
becomes my horizon

your concern
becomes my concern

and your attitude
becomes my attitude

Only then you can change
this world through me.

JOIN ME IN MY FLIGHT

Join me in my flight to the Infinite
where the sky opens, I imagine
and I, in my pain and ecstasy
with God-given might in my wings
fly into the world of peace and joy

There, shall we sit
under a blooming tree
and scribble poems
that sing of pure love

Then would you compose tunes
that touch the soul
and let the angels sing
together with the nightingales
until we fall asleep in the mystic lights
on the lap of heavenly beings
and wake up to see light pure and eternal
and smile with the joy of a little baby
at the breast of its loving mother

Would you join me now
in my flight to the Infinite?

(Poet's Note :- My heart craves for the Infinite. I am not satisfied with anything mundane. Human love lacks peace and joy which I can find only in heavenly abode on the lap of God. It is this insatiable thirst which makes me write poetry. Even in this flight to the eternal I want you to accompany me).

A THOUSAND YEARS

A thousand years are
like yesterday for you

You are the Lord of Time
The planets and stars
of the universe
revolve around you
as you deign it to be

I watch in the night
looking up to skies
how you roam about
among galaxies
and look at me
praying to you
in this dark night
from the mountains

of Sinai

TEN STRINGED LUTE

Please play on the harp

On the ten-stringed lute
let me play songs of love

I want to sing a new song
praising the glories of God

God fills the earth with his love
God fills all hearts with his love

All souls who live in this world
come with me to sing tonight
the songs of beauty and love

Beauty that shines in your heart
when you sing for your God
is the sign that He thinks
of you and your song.

[Editor's Note :- Ten strings refer to the ten sense organs (indriya) as per Yoga philosophy. There are five knowledge or "entry" senses (Jnana Indriyas) viz Sight (eyes), Hearing (ears), Smell (nose), Taste (tongue) and Touch (skin). Besides there are five action or "exit" senses (Karma Indriyas) viz Speech (mouth), Obtainment (arms), Movement (legs), Procreation (genitals) and Excretion (anus).]

GIVE ME A NEW SONG

Give me a new song

Ask your angels to come
to my soul's secret cave
to teach me a new song

I shall learn your song
from the angels' lips
kneeling at their feet
and I shall sing it slowly
in your sacred sanctuary
lighting a bright new lamp
with oil flowing from my heart
burning with the shame
of my poverty

I am poor, Lord
but i know
you will like my song
and my lamp of love.

LORD I SEE YOU DANCE

No one watches you
still you like to dance

No one listens to you
still you want to sing

No one notices you
and still you want to love

Killing all human desires
all cravings all expectations
you go on living in bliss
in your world of dreams

What a wonderful world
living in the bliss of God !!

BIRD OF MOUNT SUMERU

Far away, to the north of Sumeru
in dazzling colours of purple
stands a magnificent mountain
of many majestic peaks of gold

Four of the peaks are so lovely
my soul was love enraptured

On each peak stood a tree
with spreading dark canopy
a banyan, a pippala, a pakara
and a fruit giving mango

On top of the mountain sparkled
a beautiful lake mirroring the sky
with bejeweled flights of steps
which was delightful to behold

Its water was cool and limpid
with taste sweet like nectar
abundant with lovely lotuses
and flocks of white swans
of many different colours
uttering melodious notes
while bees softly murmured

On this splendid mountain
dwelt that deathless bird
the ageless Kaka Bhushundi
since aeons and aeons.

(Poet's Note :- Story from Ramayana Uttara Kand. A request to all my Hindu poet
friends, correct me if I commit mistakes while writing on Hindu religious texts)

Editor's Note :- Hemangi Sharma (aka Anthony) herself was born in a Hindu
Brahmin family and she is quite well versed in Hindu scriptures.

ANGELA OF FOLIGNO DREAMT

Eyes of my soul were opened
I beheld the plenitude of God
whereby I saw the whole world
both here and beyond the sea
and the Abyss and all things else

And therein did I behold naught
save the divine power all pervading
in a manner assuredly indescribable
so that through excess of marveling
my soul cried with a loud voice, saying
'This whole world is full of God!'

Wherefore did I now comprehend
that the world is but a small thing
that power of God was above all things
and that whole world was filled with it

Then He said unto me:
'I have now shown thee
something of My Power'

And I did so well understand
that it only enabled me better
to understand all other things.

And then He said to me:
"I have made thee to see
something of My Power"

'Behold now, and see My humility'.
Then was I given so deep an insight
into the utter humility of God
towards man and all other things

that when my soul remembered
His unspeakable power over all
and comprehended His humility
it did marvel greatly
and did esteem itself
to be nothing at all.

AM I A CHRISTIAN

If I affirm myself
as a Christian
merely
by denying all
that is Muslim, Jewish,
Protestant, Hindu,
Buddhist, Zoroastrian
and all other religions,
then in the end
I will find
there is
not much left
for me
to affirm
as a Christian
and certainly
no breath of the Spirit
with which
to affirm it.

(Poet's Note :- In this wonderful account, unique in the literature of mysticism, Angela of Foligno has reported the lucid vision in which she perceived this truth: the two fold apprehension of an Absolute at Once humble and omnipotent, personal and transcendent. Taken from Visionum et instructionum Liber, Chapter. xxii., English translation, P-172) .

GOD WILL LIVE AMONG MEN

The day is coming
when Lord Himself
will live with men
and they will all
be His people
and He will be
their God.

And believe me
the day is coming
like light before dawn
I can see the signs

This will be a day
when all wrongs
are put right

Joy will replace sorrow
poverty will go away
there will be richness
in all human hearts
kindness and love

and God Himself will dry
every teardrop.

INNERMOST SPACE

Only when my whole being is silent
God will enter the depth of my being
God will be born in me
in the innermost space of silence

I begin to perceive and sense
the presence of God
in my secret innermost cave

In my silence I descend
to my own inner depths

The way to the inner depths goes
through the night of my darkness
through the night of my fears
through the night of my loneliness
and my solitude born of love

There I incline myself
and lean towards
the ground of my soul

God's divine birth in me
happens in benevolent silence.

MIRACLE SONGS

Sing to me, love
the tone of Love
the miracle songs
of connections
and relationships

The tone of love
I send to you
will create
waves of love in you

It will transform you
fill you, replenish you
help you in dealing
with relationships
in family and kinship
between partners
and friends

Do create harmony
in relationships
with the tone
of my love

Help others to love
all fellow beings
remove all hatred
from the face of earth
work with all humans
like an arm of God.

JESUS IS NOT A CHRISTIAN

Jesus is not Christian
Jesus is not a Hindu
Jesus is not a Muslim
Jesus is not a Buddhist
Jesus is not monopoly
of any religion at all

Jesus is universal.
Jesus is beyond
all world religions
Jesus is eternal

He died on the Cross
He died a terrible death
To lift up the whole creation
Into benevolent presence
of Truth and only Truth
Who is God the Almighty

This universal Jesus
I love, and I love all religions
It is my consolation
and I live life joyously
singing my own psalms
coined in soulful prayer
I murmur them day and night
and I smile a beautiful smile

This faith alone makes me happy
and it is true, I am always happy.

(Poet's Note :- I am presenting an idea and did not care much about the poetic
quality here)

WHERE WILL MY SOUL GO

At the moment of my death,
where will my soul go?

Will it go to the land of the dead
or to the lap of God?

Will it enter the darkness
or the land of light?

Will it fly to the full moon
or to the land of roses
and colored peacocks?

Will my soul sing
all along the way
like a nightingale?

or will it dance with angels,
fairies and saints
drunk in the joy of God?

IF YOU DIE BEFORE ME

If you die before me
I would jump down into your grave
and hug you so innocently
that angels will become jealous

I shall kiss you
So intimately shall I kiss you
that your breath becomes mine
In one breath of love shall
we merge into hugs of true joy

Your heart shall beat
in rhythms unheard
like the drums of the desert
and the wild forest in the night

You shall murmur in my ears:
'Oh press me to your chest;
Tear open your chest,
Make way for me
to enter into your loving heart
that beats only for me
in resounding colors

Tell me please O my lover
Is it a rainbow that I see?
or the glow of a burning pyre?
Why is it that I cannot utter it in words?
Tell me O glorious angels of love :
What am I experiencing now
in these uncountable moments
of indescribable inner comfort?

Shivering in your presence
I shall long to dance with you
If the dark souls lead you to Hades
I will dance and dance with you
even in the nether world

We shall dance soft and then wild
We shall dance together
as one body and soul
and break the fetters of hell
through love that emanates from our dance

Dance so long and fine like a poem
until the Lords of the Dark would faint

Breaking the fetters of Hades
the white angels attired in beauty
shall fly down to pick you up
on their golden cradles
and carry you to the world of God

So you will be free and fly away
from me into the world of heavens
where angels shall kiss your sacred body
You will be attired in gold and white
and in varied colors in tune
with the flowers of heaven

Then you need no space to live and breathe

Into that world of purity you will go
and I will be here on earth
dreaming of your joys with
the Heavenly spirits

Shall I wait?

Shall I wait at dusk and dawn
in sobs and a heaving heart
with such desire and passion
to reach you one day
in your world of happiness.

(Poet's Note :- It is the belief that once your lady love dies before you, she has to go to the Hades and there she has to dance so fiercely and lovingly to make the Lords of Darkness faint and then she shall be free from the chains of hell. Here the living lover is ready to go to hell to dance with her most fiercely and save her from the hell)

EPILOGUE

HEMANGI SHARMA

AS ANTONY THEODORE

I AM NOT FAKE

My dear poet friend
It is not a fake ID
Only my pseudonym
And I am not theoretical poet
I am a class one English poet
Though an unconventional poet
And an off the cuff instant poet
Name and fame I do not care
I am already published
In many languages
In many formats

Shakespeare was not dear
A follower like you poet
He was a poem in flow
You must have your own DNA
To become a poet of substance
I have been to a poetry academy
Where they stripped me nude
And now my poems they salute

HEMANGI SHARMA

AS DR ANTONY THEODORE

It was in the year 2007 when for the first time I noticed certain unusual activities in the internet. Social media posts by different persons with different IDs had the same underlying pattern and digital footprint. When I tried to follow some of these posts, I started receiving similar posts in my e-mail ID as spam messages. Although I found it quite baffling, I thought it could be just a coincidence.

In 2009 a woman started stacking me online and also over phone. I received a series of calls from a woman claiming to be Swapna from Bangalore. Sometimes the woman told me that she was working as an executive at Google India office, while at other times she said she was working at Facebook. The woman started calling me from different phone numbers, each time giving a different name such as Swapna, Jyoti, Kiran, Savita etc. It was quite obvious that it was the same woman, since the voice, accent, style and intonation was the same. It was also obvious that she was stalking me for an ulterior motive, since a Google or Facebook executive would have little to do with someone like me who had hardly any presence on social media.

During the years 2011 and 2012 there was a marked reduction in the stalking activity of this woman. So I had largely forgotten aouut those spam calls and messages. But then suddenly in September 2013 a woman named Chitrangdha K Ganesh sent me a message on Poemhunter website. The title of her message read "I am bowled over by your poetic skills". It was very perplexing. I

In August 2013 I had exposed certain fraudulent activities in the online Poemhunter Poetry Competition, in which I was a participant. I found that out of the 100 poems reaching the final, 37 appeared to be the works of same person. The poems showed exquisite craftsmanship and were on wide ranging topics. But all these 37 poems had a typical signature style.

Many of these poems had been submitted by poets with similar names such as Prem Kumar, Prem Jyot, Prem123 etc. I had lodged a written complaint with Poemhunter.com website regarding such fraud, but received no response.

When I received the mail from Chitrangdha initially I thought as if the sender had some divine connection with me. But immediately I remembered the Poemhunter fraud, and thought this woman could be connected with that episode. Either the woman herself was the fraudster, or maybe some Poemhunter staff investigating the fraud. So I was wary of disclosing any details about me to this woman.

Although initially I avoided the woman, she kept on sending me her e-mail IDs and mobile numbers, requesting me to share my contact details. Although I was wary of the woman, finally curiosity got the better of me. I did some online chatting with the woman on Poemhunter platform. She introduced herself to me as a freelance worker in the field of advertisement and tourism. However after some time she started contradicting her own statements. Sometimes she said she was a researcher, a student, and IT professional or even a journalist. Sometimes she said she was married, and sometimes unmarried. Sometimes she said she was 39 years old, and at other times 33 or 43.

In April-May 2014 "Chitrangdha" obtained from me my mobile number and called me. In her very first call she told me about her life-long desire to study the Rg Veda and Qu'ran. She also told me that one day she would like to come to my house to study the Veda and Qu'ran with me. I found it quite surprising. Because ever since my childhood I had an unusual interest in the scriptures, and I had particular fascination for the rhythmic mantras of Rg Veda and Sama Veda as well as for the melodious Ayats of Quran as rendered by the Muezzins in mosques.

I developed a very intimate online relationship with this Chitrangdha. She was the first person with whom I had any personal chats online. She exchanged hundreds of messages with me via Facebook, WhatsApp,

Poemhunter, SMS and other media. Sometimes she would call me up to ten times in a day. Often she told me that it was her life-long desire to come to my house and spend the rest of her life with me. I found t very strange. I suspected of a past life connection with her.

On June 5, 2015 Chitrangdha revealed to me that her actual name was Hemangi Sharma, and that she was a student at National Institute of Rural Development, Hyderabad. She also admitted that she had been trolling me since 2009 under a series of fake IDs. She said she came to know about me from a person named Basant Kumar Rath, a senior police officer posted in Jammu. This Basant Rath was my childhood friend and had studied with me in the same class up to university level. Hemangi Sharma aka Chitrangdha had been born and brought up in Jammu before she moved to Bangalore and Hyderabad for job.

In July 2015 I met Hemangi Sharma at her office in Hyderabad. She had invited me to participate in the annual convocation ceremony of her institute. She had booked a room for me in her office guest house. I spent two days with her. During those two days she shared with me her life story. She also discussed the hidden secrets of various world scriptures including the Bible and the Qu'ran. The religious philosophies that Hemangi Sharma discussed with me are the same that Antony Theodore has described in detail in his Christian poems.

When I met Hemangi Sharma in person she did not admit that she was Antony Theodore. But she admitted that she had hundreds of fake IDs. She showed me how she had created multiple Ids by using different mobile phones and SIM cards. But when I asked her to open Chitrangdha's e-mail, she said she had forgotten Chitra's password. When I asked her why she had opened so many fake IDs, she said that she had worked as a marketing executive at Google and Facebook, and that sending spam advertisements to unsuspecting customers was part of her lucrative corporate job. She also said that she had got fed up with that kind of artificial and unethical job, and therefore she had quit the job to pursue a career in rural development.

Initially Hemangi Sharma had shared with me those IDs through whch she had been sending spam mails. But after I came back from Hyderabad, Hemangi Sharma gradually revealed to me her other IDs under which she had posted thousands of poems online. Then only I realised Hemangi Sharma's true stature as a world class poet. I was surprised that she had not published even a single poem under her own name. All her poems had been published under hundreds of pseudonyms. After introducing me to her poetry, Hemangi Sharma deactivated her original e-mail IDs. So I was forced to correspond with her via her fake IDs. She discussed her poetry with me in great detail over thousands of messages exchanged through such fake IDs. And then one fine day she deleted all her messages to me. That left me with no evidence that she had indeed discussed her poetry with me. However I managed to save a few of those messages as proof of her correspondence with me.

Hemangi Sharma has uploaded thousands of her poems in different languages under hundreds of fake IDs. She is a multi-linguist with scholarly understanding of all major world religions. One fails to understand why a spiritual person like her would use so many fake IDs, which is clearly a criminal offence. But then strange are the ways of the devotees of God.

When Hemangi Sharma first started corresponding with me, I immediately knew that she was the person behind the hundreds of fake IDs under which she had uploaded her poems. However she admitted to it much later, only after I relentlessly pursued her to know the truth. She has the talent and creativity to write spontaneously in thousands of different styles. But there were certain underlying patterns in all her works. The most common element in her writings is her use of small "i" to denote the first person singular. She purportedly did so to underplay the individual ego in the creative process. But there is still no plausible explanation for the use of thousands of fake IDs. She could have adopted a single pseudonym to mask her identity, but she chose to have thousands. I believe that she wrote under fake IDs to completely dissociate her ego from the creative process. I myself had resorted to such a technique during my student days. I found that the poems I had written under pseudonyms were qualitatively much better than those published under my real name.

Another underlying pattern in Hemangi Sharma's writings is her utter disregard for the conventional rules of grammar. Among all her online avatars, I found Dr Tony Brahmin (Antony Theodore) as comparatively the most conventional one in terms of style. Still certain poetic freedom can be seen by discerning readers.

Yet another frequent feature in Hemangi Sharma's writings is the use of abbreviations, colloquial expressions and liberal use of nouns as verbs and adjectives. For instance she would write "RV Lovers" instead of "Are We in Love". You is abbreviated to "u" in most of her writings. Instead of "more childish", she will simply write "childer". For instance, in one of her letters to me, she wrote "love makes heart become childer". Even mobile SMS texts such as Gn and Tc (goodnight, take care etc) frequently appear in her poems. She also uses past, present and future tenses in the same poem as part of the same dialogue between protagonists. This reflects her belief that time is an illusion, and that earthly concept of time does not exist at all in the realm of God consciousness.

What makes her art so special is that she makes such unusual expressions quite spontaneously. The reader hardly suspects that she is deliberately doing so.

In addition to "Antony", Hemangi Sharma has also adopted other interesting pseudonyms such as Lalitha Iyer, Dev Anand, Poet Poet, Sun Princess, April Pearl and a host of other IDs. She has used both male and female names, as well as names from different languages. She has used Hindu names, Christian names and Muslim names. Maybe she did so to identify herself with all humanity irrespective of artificial barriers created by gender, race, caste, language and religion.

But still she could have managed to do all this with 30 or 40 IDs. I really don't know what could have been Hemangi Sharma's real intention in adopting hundreds and thousands of fake IDs. Any discerning reader would have noticed the underlying pattern in the poems written under different IDs. But perhaps nobody pointed it out before I did so. I was the only person who lodged a written complaint regarding her fake IDs. Perhaps Hemangi Sharma deliberately did so with the expectation that someday someone would find out her real identity. Perhaps it was God's design that I would become that person. Or maybe it was Hemangi Sharma's own design – who knows?

Hemangi Sharma had frequently expressed to me her desire to open a school for underprivileged children, and also to adopt a baby girl with my financial support. She wanted to have an unconventional school, which would be completely free from the curriculum of rote learning. She told me that she wanted me as the Mentor of her "school". I do not know what exactly was in my mind. I asked her to explain to me her idea of "mentor". But she was evasive in her answers. However, from the very beginning of her interactions with me she clearly told me about her disapproval of abortion of foetuses. Protection of children and their precious childhood was her topmost priority, and it took up bulk of her conversations with me. She said she had left her lucrative corporate job to take up the study of rural development solely for the purpose of empowering vulnerable women and underprivileged children. But that still does not explain her thousands of fake IDs and deliberate lies. Why should a spiritual person tell such lies?

Hopefully Hemangi Sharma (Antony Theodore) herself will one day provide answers to all these unanswered questions.

Tapan Kumar Pradhan

www.ingramcontent.com/pod-product-compliance
Lightning Source LLC
LaVergne TN
LVHW020319200726
843507LV00012B/2166

9 788194 283539